Lazuli Finch
JOHN J. AUDUBON

FROM THE BOOKS OF

" *Jean B.* "

The
NEEDLEWORK
BOOK

by Wanda Passadore

CONTENTS

THE ART OF CROCHET   113

KNITTING 161

PLEASURES OF NEEDLEWORK

Popular as it has been throughout the ages, needlework today has tremendous appeal, as much for the relaxation it affords—it is harmonious and peaceful work—as for the satisfactions of creating lastingly beautiful things whose value grows with the years. Today's needlework is tomorrow's heirloom.

In this book we have concentrated on the kinds of stitches and designs that offer the greatest possibilities, and we believe that the detailed photographs—*showing* every phase of the work, step-by-step—will make it possible even for beginners to execute them with ease.

EMBROIDERY

Thus we begin with embroidery suited to modern life and temperament. No one today has the time (or patience) for meticulous embroideries on fragile tulle, or the making of hand-sewn lace and other exquisite creations of earlier times. So our collection of embroidery stitches, wide as it is, has been limited to the most attractive examples within the capabilities of the amateur.

Canvas embroidery—most soothing of work—is deservedly enjoying a new wave of popularity. Our designs, ranging from fine petit point to hooked Persian rugs, can give a delightful handmade touch to any style of decor.

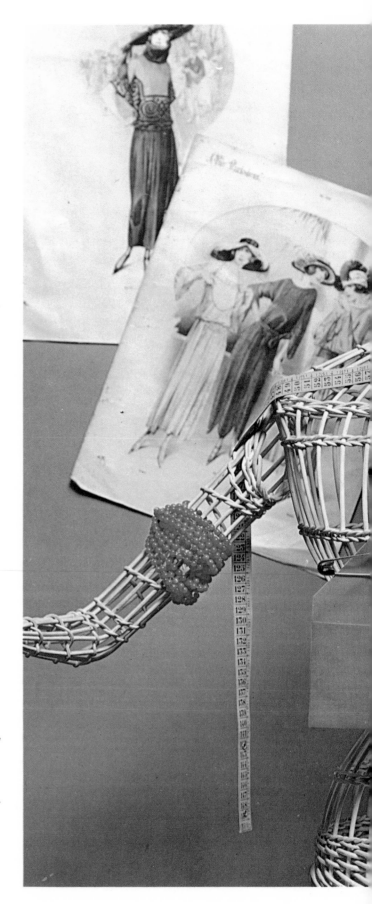

CROCHET AND KNITTING

Here too, work has been chosen for the freshness with which it applies the traditional skills to modern styles. The range is vast, the skills themselves so enjoyable, and the results are bound to give pleasure.

The many stitches presented here can be adapted to all kinds of work—whether heirloom bedspreads or modern table mats, baby christening dresses or bulky sportswear. And the styles are those that will endure.

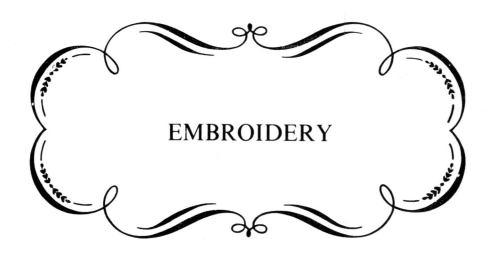

EMBROIDERY

The first steps in learning embroidery technique must be devoted to such basic preliminaries as choosing embroidery materials and threads, preparation of the material and methods of reproducing and enlarging designs. It is also important to understand the uses of the frame, which is necessary for perfect execution of many kinds of embroidery.

Once these principles are understood, we begin with the stitches themselves. We hope to show that beautiful embroidery need not be difficult—indeed, some of the most charming effects come from imaginative use of even the simplest of stitches.

SELECTING THE FABRIC

The choice of fabric will usually determine the kind of stitch (or stitches) to be executed, and the style of the finished product, as well. There are many fabrics available today—one can embroider on canvas, on silk, on tulle and organdy, on terry cloth and cottons, including many new drip-dry materials—but the most popular of all is linen. Linen is perhaps easiest to embroider, and its freshness and crisp texture enhance every type of work.

For those for whom embroidery is a hobby rather than a profession, the following types of fabrics are the most useful:

Lightweight fabrics

Lightweight cottons and linens are best for delicate stitches like the shadow stitch, four-sided stitch and satin stitch. (Numbers 1, 2 and 3 in the photo opposite.)

Medium and heavyweight fabrics

Linen, butcher linen, fine burlap, sampler linen and a variety of the new cotton-rayon mixtures are ideal for the more substantial stitches, which work more rapidly. (Numbers 4, 5 and 6, opposite.)

Canvas

There is a wide and interesting range of canvases available. Penelope canvas is woven in many different weights and textures, each having a different number of threads to the inch which greatly facilitates the counting of threads while embroidering. (See opposite: number 7 for classic cross stitch; 8 for petit-point; 9 for needlepoint; 10 and 11 for Smyrna cross-stitch and hand knotted rugs.)

How to iron embroidery

Embroidery must always be ironed on the wrong side. Place a double thickness of turkish toweling over a regulation padded ironing board and spread the dampened fabric over it, right side down. Use heavy pressure on the iron, taking care to stroke horizontally and vertically along the exact grain lines of the fabric. Any pressure on the bias will result in a misshapen, puckered motif. Never iron embroidery on the right side, as the iron will flatten the threads and ruin the texture so painstakingly accomplished.

Embroidery done on canvas should never be pressed.

EMBROIDERY THREAD

The choice of thread also plays a very important role in the finished effect of your work; it can be clear or soft, bright or dull, compact or transparent. Each type of thread is suited to a particular group of stitches, and all must be in proper relation to the fabric used.

Mouline cotton

This is the most versatile and widely used embroidery thread. It is popularly known as six-strand thread and easily separates into groups of 2, 3, or 4 strands, depending upon the requirements of a particular stitch. It is bright, suitable for "classic" embroideries, and for such basic stitches as satin stitch, padded stitch, etc. (A in the picture on this page.)

Perle cotton

This is the traditional name for a twisted thread popularly known as tatting or crochet-sheen. It comes in different weights for use on textured stitches. It is most suitable for chain stitch, Palestrina stitch, bokhara couching, split stitch, filling stitch, stem stitch, etc. (In picture: C, D, F.)

Embroidery cotton

This is a thinner thread than those above, not as twisted, and the strands are not separable. It is suitable for scalloping and smocking stitches, and for open crochet work.

Woolen thread and tapestry yarn

These yarns are used mainly for canvas works, but may also be used for the running stitch, chain stitch or split stitch when a particular texture is required. They are slightly twisted yarns which do not ravel easily when passing through the canvas holes, come in a variety of soft shades, and cover the work with thick, compact stitches. (In the picture: B, E, and G.)

While a few stitches are easily worked in the hand, such as the stem stitch, lazy daisy, turkish stitch, and bokhara couching, others require the use of a frame for perfect results. Adjusting to the slight difference caused by the use of the frame is simple, and both the round Swiss frame and the larger, adjustable rectangular frame prove to be indispensable once they are tried.

With an embroidery frame there is no idle hand—both hands work. The right hand inserts the needle into the work; the left hand (which is kept under the frame) pulls the needle through to the back and re-inserts it in the cloth, from which it emerges on the right side to complete the stitch. This is only a small change from normal sewing habits and results in enjoyable, rhythmic work.

The round frame

This consists of two wooden hoops attached to a base which can be held on the knee while leaving the hands free to work. To use this frame, remove the larger (outside) hoop; place the material over the smaller hoop attached to the base, making certain that the grain line of the material is exactly straight with the vertical and horizontal lines of the frame. When replacing the larger hoop, carefully stretch the material, keeping the grain lines at perfect right angles to each other. This prevents a misshapen design when it is removed from the frame. Another important precaution is to calculate in advance the distance between the various motifs, so that previously embroidered sections do not fall within the grip of the two hoops.

If the embroidery has a continuous border, or if it covers the entire surface of the fabric, it is necessary to use the rectangular frame.

The rectangular frame

The rectangular frame is easily dismantled into four compact little bars that can be stored in a drawer. A strong tape is nailed to two of these wooden bars, and two sides of the embroidery cloth are overcast onto these. The other two bars, which have holes at regular intervals, are then set into the slots of the first two bars. Before firmly anchoring these side bars with the wooden pegs provided, the material must be stretched properly. The most practical system is to pin the selvage of the cloth and with a strong thread work a zig-zag between the side bar and the pins (see diagram). This simple process takes little time and results in much easier performance.

In the picture opposite: a rectangular frame. On this page, to the left: detail of rectangular frame; above: the round frame.

HOW TO REPRODUCE DESIGNS

Before embroidering it is necessary to reproduce the design accurately on the cloth. Obviously, poorly prepared work with a crooked or irregular design will spoil the final result, even if embroidered with utmost skill. The three following methods of transferring designs to cloth have been tried and tested by long experience.

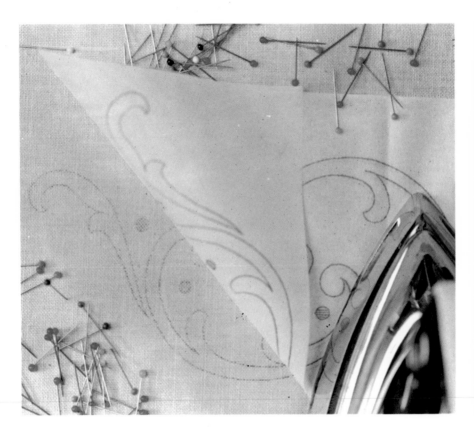 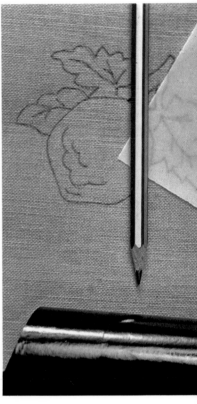

Hot-iron transfers

Designs which have been prepared with special inks are available in fabric shops or needlework sections of department stores. Place the chosen motif on the fabric, then press it with a hot iron; the iron should be placed firmly on each part of the motif and then lifted. No strokes should be made (this prevents streaking). The design, melted by the heat, is transferred neatly and perfectly to the cloth. This method, although quick and easy, is generally limited to a few dozen traditional designs available.

Transferring with carbon paper

If you wish to copy a design found in a magazine or book, you can use a very simple method using the special fabric carbon paper found in needlework sections of shops and department stores. You must first trace the design on strong, transparent tracing paper. The next step is to place the carbon paper on the cloth, and position on it the traced design. Transfer this onto the cloth, using a pencil (not too pointed) and a light hand. Never use a pen. This system is excellent for scattered motifs, less advisable for designs that cover large surfaces and require symmetry and absolute perfection.

Transferring with a perforated pattern

This method, although more detailed, has a definite advantage—the same design may be reproduced innumerable times, each time identical. Carefully trace the chosen motif in the center of a sheet of strong tracing paper (motif must be centered to avoid unwanted spots in the next step). Then place the tracing on the ironing board and patiently perforate the entire contour with pinholes spaced 1/8 inch apart.

Preparation of the material

Regardless of the transfer method you choose, the embroidery cloth must first be accurately measured off to receive the design. After cutting the cloth to desired dimensions, determine the center by folding the cloth into four parts (on the straight grain) and mark the folds with a warm iron. If

Place this pattern on the embroidery cloth and brush lightly over the perforations with a soft pad saturated with powdered tailor's chalk—either blue or white, whichever gives a contrasting color. When finished, spray lightly with alcohol to set the chalk marks and allow to dry thoroughly. If you wish to set the motifs with a hot iron instead of with alcohol, place a sheet of clean tissue paper between the cloth and iron before pressing, taking great care not to streak the design.

If the embroidery cloth is lightweight, and the design must consequently be very light, place the pattern with the rough side of the perforations against the cloth. For a heavier cloth and a heavily marked design, place the smooth side against the cloth.

necessary, eight folds may be used. These folds divide the work into equal segments to be used both for scattering motifs with a certain regularity, and to control the pattern repeat of a continuous border.

It is always advisable to scale the border pattern to the size of a repeat. In each case, an extremely practical method is to pin one end of a tape measure to the center of the work and slowly rotate from this pivot point, marking the position of the motifs or border widths at the chosen distance.

Far left picture: transferring a design with a hot iron; center: with tracing paper; on the right: with a perforated pattern.

How to enlarge designs

At times the design you wish to copy is photographed on too small a scale. How can you scale it to the desired size? The method is simple. First, trace the design on a piece of tracing paper. Enclose the design within a square. With carbon paper, transfer this square and the design to a piece of graph paper. (Available in most stationary departments.)

You must now determine exactly how much you wish to enlarge the design, and on a piece of unlined paper draw a square to the desired size. Count and number the blocks of your small design as illustrated below; with a sharp pencil and straight ruler mark off and number the same amount of vertical and horizontal lines on the larger square on plain paper. Patiently copy your design on the larger scale, block by block; practice will enable you to do this easily.

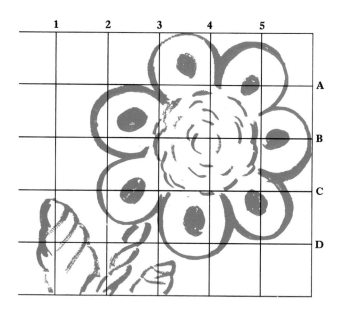

STEM STITCH OR OUTLINE STITCH

This is the easiest of all embroidery stitches, originally used only for flower stems and to outline the veining of leaves. However, with time, it has acquired a history and dignity of its own, so that today you will find it not only in simple compositions, but also in combination with much fancier stitches on very luxurious fabrics. Twisted threads are best suited for this stitch to clearly detail its simple construction.

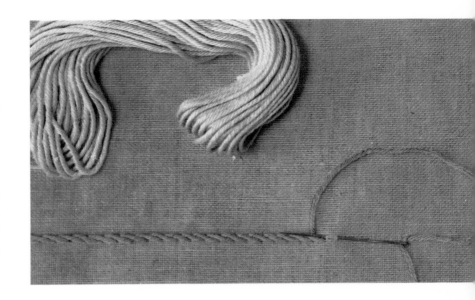

THE LAZY DAISY STITCH

This is another of the very simple stitches, used to embroider daisies and small leaves; rarely used in sophisticated compositions. Yet, it has a decorative grace of its own, reminiscent of early school days; in fact, to this day it is usually a little girl's first experience with embroidery.

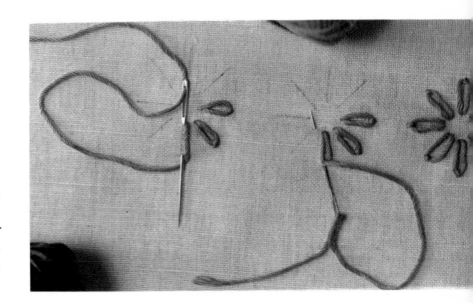

How to make the stem stitch

The line on which the stem stitch is to be used is rarely straight, as it generally follows curves and circles within the design. It is therefore impossible to establish a stitch length by counting threads; experience will teach you to judge this at sight. Work from left to right, holding the thread above the sketched line in the material, and take short even stitches from right to left bringing the needle out on the line the work is to follow. (Top photo.)

How to make a lazy daisy stitch

Bring the needle up from the wrong side at the top of the stitch and draw the thread through. Use left thumb to hold thread down in a loop. Reinsert the needle at the same place and take a stitch catching the thread under the needle. Draw the thread through to form a loop. Fasten this loop by inserting needle just outside it. Bring needle up again at center of the flower for next petal. (Lower photo.) Thread is fastened off after completing last petal.

Is an embroidery frame necessary?

The embroidery frame is essential for perfect tension on the stitches, which could otherwise be too tight and pull the fabric underneath, or be too loose. The large rectangular frame provides for wide visual range when working on large border patterns of flowers and leaves which are so beautiful and popular today.

For the breakfast table, a colorful and easy embroidery: it is entirely stem stitch and lazy daisy stitch worked with mouline thread (large photo). Details are shown in the small photos.

THE BLANKET STITCH

This is the stitch used at one time to trim miles and miles of buttonholes on generations of blouses and pillow cases. But it is also a true embroidery stitch, to be used alone or in combination with others. Its function is to give finishing touches and emphasis wherever a strong outline is needed.

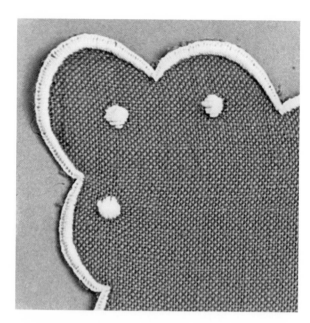

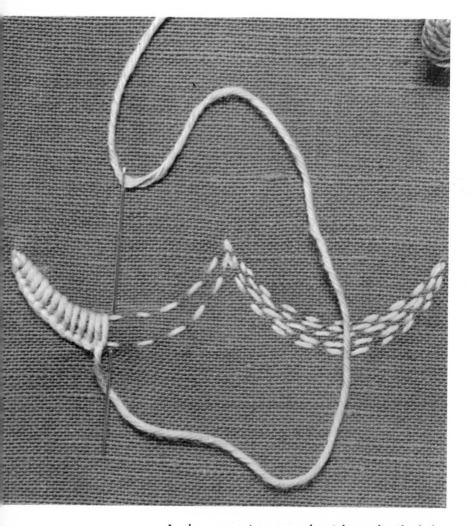

In the upper picture, to the right: a detail of the place mat shown opposite. Directly above: on the grey-green fabric, the work method for the blanket stitch. Shown are the two types of underlining—at left: the stitch is worked over a simple outline; at right: the outline is padded with lines of running stitches. Opposite: a place mat of heavy blue linen, with scalloped edges done in blanket stitch. The line of the border is emphasized with dots made in satin stitch.

Where and how to use it

Blanket stitch is much used for scalloped edges, singly or in groups; it may be raised by padding underneath with small running stitches. Used by itself, it can give elegance to the most simple tablecloth or bedspread.

This is a stitch that requires great accuracy in execution. Stitch length and the distance between stitches must be regular; they must be very close but not overlapping. And for scalloping they must follow the half-moon outline exactly. After embroidering scalloped edges, care must also be taken in trimming away the excess material. Use very sharp, bent scissors, and work accurately to avoid cutting into the stitches, as they cannot be repaired.

The design

Since the beauty of blanket stitch depends on its regularity, and regularity begins with design, the perforated pattern is the most advisable method of reproducing it. Prepare a design on tracing paper, covering at least five or six scallops if they continue in a straight line, or groups of two or three if they are to be curved or joined to form a large edging. Before transferring the design to the fabric, you must first establish the shape of each corner and the number of scallops to fit on each side.

Another easy method is to take a piece of cardboard and draw several scallops on it, tracing around a coin, or a glass or cup (depending on size wanted). Then trim away the cardboard around the outer edges of the scallops and use as a pattern.

The thread

It is important to choose a twisted thread (mouline, perle) which will not ravel or knot in mid-scallop. Calculate in advance the length of thread needed to complete a scallop, as interruptions to start a new thread will invariably show and break the continuity of the scallop.

How to work the blanket stitch

The first step is to prepare the outline for the stitch to follow: this is done with two lines of running stitch. If you wish to raise (or pad) the stitch, full in the space within the outline with small running stitches.

In either case, embroider as follows: starting from the left, insert the needle downwards, while holding the thread under the left thumb. Bring the needle out over the thread, then allow thread to flow through easily, stopping it with your thumb to make the resulting knot. The scallop is perfect when stitches are neither loose nor tight. (If tight, the material will curl around the scallops, and even ironing will not flatten it.)

THE DOUBLE BLANKET STITCH

This is an interesting variation which deserves to be used much more often than it is. Executed in the same way as blanket stitch, it gives a totally different effect. Instead of outlining the edges, double blanket stitch is used in the body of the work. It is a "covering" stitch, which can fill in designs in a quick and uncomplicated way, while clearly defining the contour as well.

Obviously, it is best suited to linear forms in small areas. Extremely easy and enjoyable to do, double blanket stitch is highly effective and recommended even for beginners.

The design

Transferring patterns can be done by any method. However, for lightweight fabrics the hot iron method is advisable; the perforated pattern sprayed with alcohol is excellent on heavier fabrics.

The thread

As with blanket stitch, you need a twisted thread that will not ravel. Embroidery cotton is very good for this; perle is excellent. The thickness will be determined by the firmness of the basic fabric.

A particularly successful application of double blanket stitch: observe here how it brightly and lightly traces a group of small leaves, with the help of a stem stitch. Most unusual are the flower petals embroidered in single blanket stitch around small holes previously made with a bodkin.

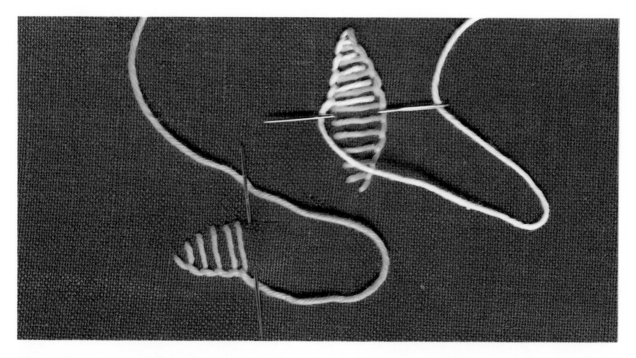

Above: the two phases of double blanket stitch. First the yellow thread, starting from the left, designs the shape of the leaf. Then the fabric is reversed, and the white thread fills in the spaces between the stitches of the first group, completing the design. Below: a detail of the place mat shown on the previous page.

How to work the double blanket stitch

Work from right to left, in blanket stitch, inserting the needle downward, exactly on the upper and lower edges of the design, and bringing it out over the thread. Do not space the stitches closely—between each stitch, leave a space equal to the thickness of one stitch.

Reverse the fabric and work in blanket stitch, filling in the spaces left between stitches on the first round.

Is an embroidery frame needed?

Although this can be done in the hand, the use of a frame will maintain perfect tension and help achieve a uniform and compact result. A simple round frame will do, since this type of stitch does not cover large areas. When using the frame, each stitch is completed in two stages: the right hand passes the needle down at the upper edge; then, under the frame, the left hand guides the needle up again at the lower edge just inside the thread.

THE CHAIN STITCH

The chain stitch and the Palestrina stitch (which follows later) are typical examples of knotted stitches—those which line up, one after the other, with no problems of light and shadow, of outline or thread counting. Perhaps because of its simplicity, chain stitch has long been under-valued, except as a beginner's stitch. Now that the taste for simple, graphic embroidery has returned, chain stitch has also returned to use.

It is particularly attractive for tablecloths, curtains, bedspreads, scarves, etc., often replacing old-fashioned passamenterie with its finer look. It lends itself easily to original and personalized designs.

Chain stitch is most impressive when embroidered in two, three or five lines close together, using thick white thread on a background of deep colors such as rust, forest green, tobacco, burgundy, and especially dark blue or golden yellow.

But even a single row of this versatile stitch creates a bright light of its own. A good example is illustrated on the following page, where it is displayed on a tablecloth which is both informal and elegant. The same effect can be achieved on bedspreads of any style, or on linen hand towels.

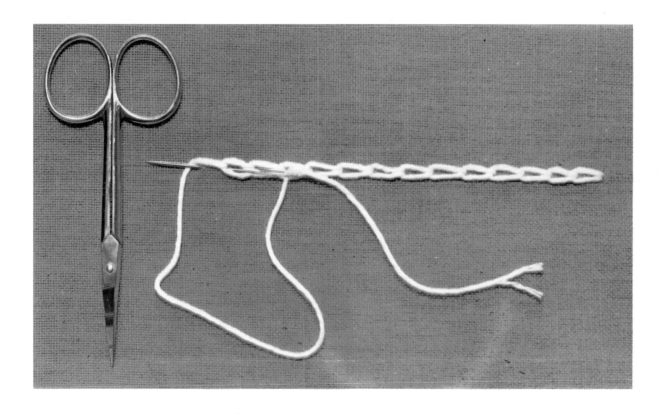

The classic chain stitch usually progresses from top to bottom, with stitches interlocking one after the other, very evenly. Once familiar with the technique, you can also embroider from right to left (as shown above).

The thread and the material

As this is a raised stitch, thicker and more prominent threads are preferable to emphasize its characteristics. Perle and woolen threads are excellent for this purpose. All kinds of materials are suit-

33

able, from heavy upholstery reps, twills and shantungs through the whole gamut of lightweight decorative cottons. Essentially casual in style, chain stitch can appear on such diverse materials as terry cloth and organdy.

The design

If you are using a scattered design, or one which does not require geometric precision, it can first be traced, then transferred to the fabric by the carbon paper method.

For a design with regular, geometric contours (as in the aqua tablecloth illustrated), it is best to draw a 1/4 or 1/8-section of the circle on a large sheet of tracing paper and then transfer to the fabric by the perforated pattern method. Place your design carefully, taking care to rotate the transfer line from the exact center of the tablecloth.

If you are making a scalloped outline with chain stitch, you can easily make a cardboard pattern for scallops as shown on page 28.

How to work the chain stitch

Working from top to bottom, bring the threaded needle through the fabric to the right side. Hold the thread down with the left thumb, and re-insert needle as close as possible to the point from which it originally emerged; then take a short stitch, bringing needle out of the fabric a short distance forward and over the thread. Thus the first link is formed. For the continuing links the needle is always re-inserted at the point where the thread emerged and brought out slightly forward. This determines the length of the stitch (which should be proportioned to thread size); it is best to keep the thread rather loose and avoid too short a stitch.

For this tablecloth, a heavy aqua linen was used with a double circle of chain stitch arabesques to underline its circular shape. Prepare a 1/4 section of the circle to reproduce the design on the fabric.

Note: Start with the length of thread necessary to finish one entire motif, thus avoiding any break in continuity.

CHAIN STITCH USING THE FRAME

When done with a frame, the chain stitch is adaptable to decidedly modern designs. Embroidered in close rows within the confines of a design (as in the large photo, page 36), it is no longer an outline stitch but takes on an entirely new characteristic as a filling stitch. Used in this way it has become one of the several most popular stitches for contemporary embroidery.

The design and the material

Although there are no specific requirements, there are certain preferences. The carbon paper method is best for reproducing the design, and its heavy marking will be well covered by the stitch. Casual fabrics—heavy cottons and linens with clearly defined threads—go well with the chain stitch.

How to embroider chain stitch on a frame

With the frame, one does not use a needle, but a fine and pointed crochet hook which will enter the cloth without making too visible a hole.

Working from right to left: with the right hand, insert the hook into the cloth. With the left hand, which holds the thread under the frame, loop the thread over the hook. With the right hand, pull the loop back through the cloth to the right side and, keeping the loop on the hook, continue to repeat this process along the line of the design.

The frame

If the area to be embroidered does not exceed 10 inches in diameter, the round frame is used. The rectangular frame is best for a larger embroidery. If the area is very large, the rectangular frame may be used on one section at a time, thus avoiding wrinkles and providing proper stretching of the fabric.

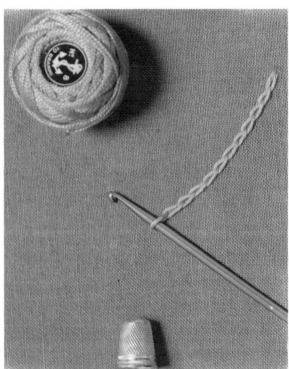

In the picture to the left: a field of abstract tulips with a stylized line and vivacious yet subtle coloring. A good pattern for a luncheon cloth, a throw pillow, or even a lampshade for a country room.
Above: the chain stitch done on a frame, with a crochet hook. It need not follow any grain of the fabric; in this case, it is worked along the bias.

COUCHING STITCH AND BOKHARA COUCHING ARE ALMOST IDENTICAL

Couching stitch is a sturdy and handsome stitch generally used to fill wide areas. It is much easier to do than it looks, and works much more swiftly than other more commonly used filling stitches, such as the satin stitch.

Couching stitch is of medieval origin, and was widely used by the ladies of the castle who devoted their time to beautiful tapestries. Today it is used to create designs with a strong play of light and shade, usually on a firm cloth.

Bokhara couching can achieve an almost 18th-century grace when delicately embroidered on the lightest of fabrics, such as organdy or linen. In bokhara couching, the lines fill the design, but do not lie too closely together.

The design

Couching stitch has no particular demands as far as reproduction is concerned; any of the transfer methods can be used.

For bokhara couching, do not transfer the outside contour of the motif. Instead, hatch the entire area within the design with light pencil marks which will be the base for the stitches.

The thread and the fabric

Couching stitch can be done on all firm materials such as linen or cotton, using twisted threads suited to filling spaces rapidly. Perle thread is ideal for this purpose.

Bokhara couching is best done on lightweight fabrics, with mouline thread (used two strands at a time).

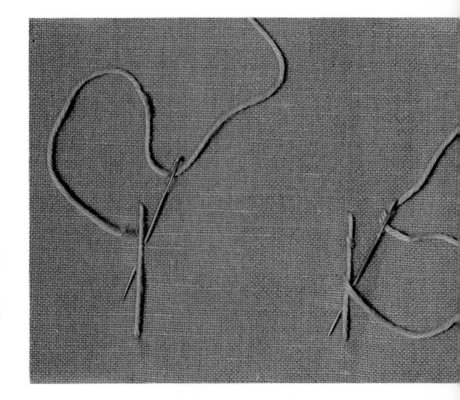

How to embroider couching stitch

Couching stitch is formed by one or more long vertical lines, closely placed, within the boundaries of the area to be filled. These lines are then fastened by a series of short, slanted stitches.

Hold the long stitch in place with the left thumb. Working from left to right, draw the needle out of the fabric on the left side of the long stitch, and re-insert the needle slightly lower on the right

Couching stitch, showing the different phases of execution. On the left: the long vertical base stitch connecting the two outer edges of the motif, and the clearly evident movement of the first slant stitch. On the right: the first completed slant stitch is seen, and the needle has re-emerged below it to form the second slant stitch. The number of slant stitches obviously depends on the length of the base thread.

side, to form the slanted stitch which completes and fastens it. In this manner, fasten the basic stitch at regular intervals, taking care not to cover it too closely. As each stitch is completed, the needle returns to the wrong side, and emerges close to it to form the next long stitch which is fastened with slanted stitches in the same way. The placement of slanted stitches should alternate with each row, to give a woven effect.

Couching stitch can be used to give varying effects of light and shadow by embroidering different areas in different directions. It is not necessary to follow the straight grain of the cloth.

Using the frame

Even though it is not essential, it is advisable to use the round frame for best results. Working with it requires only a little more time, and the ensuing perfection of work is its reward.

In the large picture in the center: color is dominant in this beautiful tablecloth of heavy cotton, in which the couching stitch, done with twisted woolen embroidery thread, fills each leaf and motif swiftly and thickly. In the two small pictures, above and to the right: details of the design. (Tablecloth by T.A.F., Florence)

How to do bokhara couching

Bokhara couching distributes its colors in a way very similar to the transparencies of water color. Consequently it requires fragile fabrics and thin threads.

The technique is identical to that of couching stitch; the only difference is slightly wider spacing between the long base threads—strictly guided by

the hatching drawn on the material—which gives an almost sketchy effect. The finished work is very light and is preferably done in pastel colors which are emphasized and intensified by the transparent, fragile style of the whole.

In the picture above: a place mat to which bokhara couching in soft shadings gives a lightness impossible to match with any other filling stitch. (Place mat by Canetta-Milan.) To the left: a detail of the same. This clearly shows the absence of a sharp outline and, when compared with the detail of the couching stitch (opposite), reveals the difference between the two stitches.

THE SIMPLE RUNNING STITCH

This is the basic embroidery stitch of all those worked by counting threads, and the execution is extremely easy. When well done, the running stitch worked in alternating rows (or in alternating long and short stitches) can produce a smooth, uniform effect equal to that of many stitches far more complicated. It gives a fresh look, adapted to modern designs, with raised textures given by thick cotton or woolen threads.
It is sometimes used with an edging of chain stitch to hide the inevitable irregularities and give a more finished look. At other times (as in the large picture, opposite), it is used by itself with clear and strong effect.

The design

For transferring patterns, a light hand is indispensable, especially if they are to be embroidered without an edging. The perforated pattern method is most suitable, as the holes can be widely spaced to leave a barely perceptible tracing on the cloth, which can be easily hidden under the stitches.

The material and the thread

There is great freedom of choice here; however, rather rough fabrics with clearly visible, easily counted threads are preferable. Any kind of thread may be used, depending on the cloth.

How to do running stitch

Running stitch is best done following the straight grain of fabric, aligning the stitches in parallel rows and spacing the rows to give a heavy or light filling, as desired. It is usually done in the hand, but a frame will allow a more even tension and more regular and controlled distance between stitches. The needle passes under one thread of the fabric and over as many as you determine, to produce the desired effect.

Basket-weave running stitch is done in rows of stitches of equal length. Alternating rows are started in mid-stitch.

Used as a filling, running stitch presents an irregular pattern in which the stitches have different lengths and may run in any direction, regardless of fabric grain, depending on the contours of the design they are filling in or accentuating. Despite the apparent freedom, this is a more difficult method, as the uncontrolled stitches have a tendency to pile up and produce thick spots in the design.

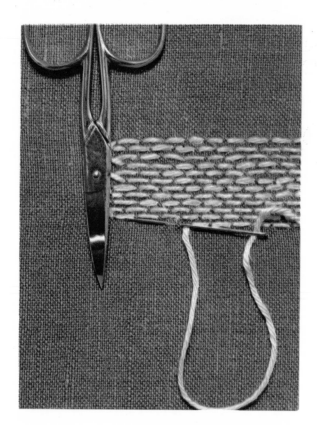

Above: the running stitch in "basket-weave" effect: all the stitches are the same length, and can be worked from right to left, or from top to bottom.

To the right: when embroidery combines with elegant design, it becomes real art. Notice the perfection of the running stitch in this table runner of rust-colored homespun material.

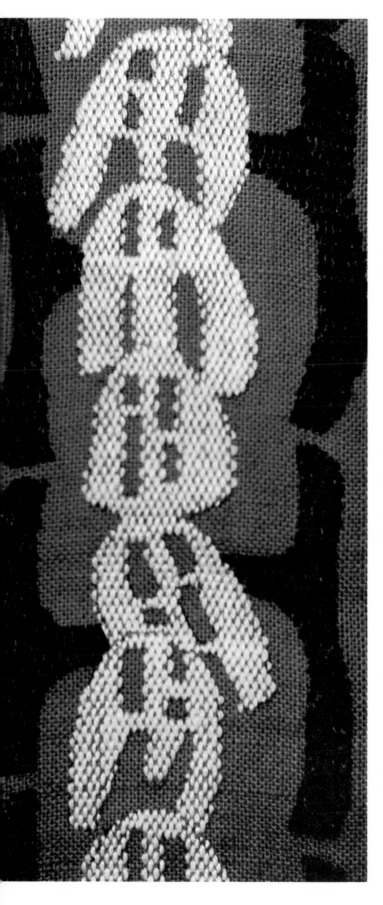
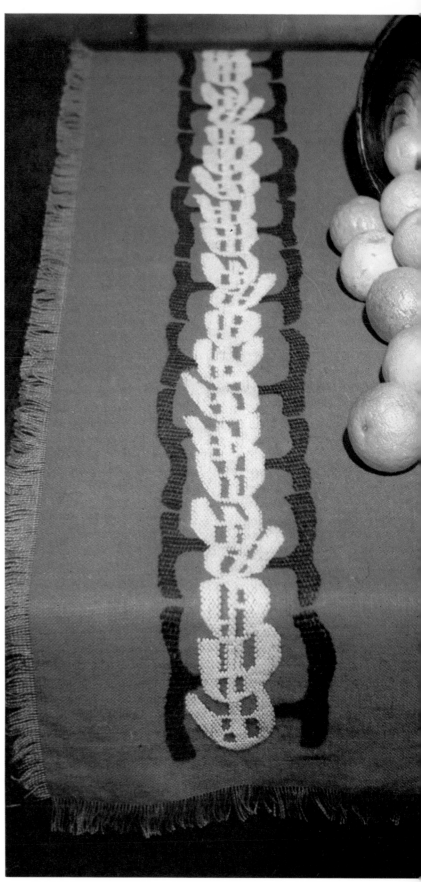

THE PALESTRINA STITCH

This stitch has a rhythm that begins, increases and ends in four movements. It is formed by a series of elaborate knots, done in orderly sequence, and following any graceful design of circles and arabesques. Once the technique is mastered, it is a totally relaxing stitch, repeated over and over until the entire design is complete. There are no threads to count, the material is firm, the thread strong and clearly visible. In fact, this is one in a small category of stitches that can be done with one eye on the work and the other on the T.V. screen. It is always used alone, and is never combined with other stitches.

The design

Since Palestrina stitch is generally used in symmetrical designs, the reproduction of the pattern presents no difficulty, as any imperfections can be corrected while embroidering. The carbon paper method is most often used.

The material and thread

Palestrina stitch is most effective when it emphasizes a clear and decorative line. Because of its thickness, it is rarely used on delicate linens, but is most often used for tablecloths, runners, bedspreads, etc. The material should be tightly woven, the thread heavily twisted to emphasize the knot. White thread is perhaps best of all, especially on a background of intense color.

How to do Palestrina stitch

Palestrina stitch is worked from left to right. Calculate the distance between stitches at approximately 5 threads, as the design rarely follows a straight line.

To begin: draw the needle out of the fabric (upper left photo, opposite) and vertically slanting up to the right, take a stitch from top to bottom.

The following phases, making the knot, are worked on the slant stitch itself without penetrating the fabric with the needle. With the thread on the right, pass the needle under the slant stitch from top to bottom (middle photo), and draw the thread through. Then pass the needle under the slant

stitch again, this time holding the thread under the needle to the left, so the needle passes over it, forming the knot (bottom photo).

Thread tension must remain loose to avoid puckering the cloth. Then continue to the next knot, with another vertically slanting stitch into the cloth.

Note: To avoid catching the fabric while making the knot, it is a good idea to use a thin tapestry needle with rounded point instead of a sharp embroidery needle. Another method is to reverse the needle—leading with the hole-end instead of the point.

A word of advice

Before starting a piece of work, a little preliminary practice on the execution of the knot will establish the length of the stitch in proportion to the cloth and thread. Most important, it will also establish the thread tension to give the best results.

At right, in the large picture: a charming curved motif embroidered with Palestrina stitch in white on turquoise—ideal for a place mat or the corners of a luncheon cloth or a telephone book cover. In the small pictures, the three phases of making the knot.

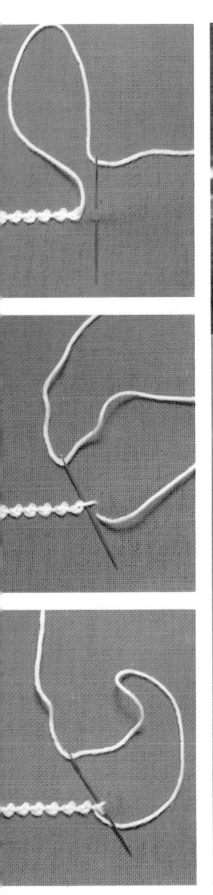

SATIN STITCH GOES
WITH EVERYTHING

One of the most representative of all the great family of embroidery stitches is the satin stitch. It has such a wide range of applications that it is suited to almost all embroidery work. The satin stitch lends itself just as easily to large areas as small ones and cheerfully adapts to any fabric from the most luxurious to the most casual.
Its style is characterized by an extreme versatility combined with a quite elementary technique, although it reveals strict precision in its execution as stitches must be perfectly aligned for clarity of contour.

The material and the thread
The choice of materials suitable for satin stitch is boundless; it lends the proper and persuasive note to anything from the finest linen through a range of fabrics to the roughest hemp. Its versatility is assisted by clear, strong threads such as the perlé for heavy fabrics and mouliné for light fabrics.

The design
There can be complete freedom of choice in reproduction of the design, since the satin stitch is almost always in the company of other stitches with well defined requirements, and will adjust to the occasional demands of its companions. However, it does show a certain preference for the perforated pattern which does not make too heavy an outline.

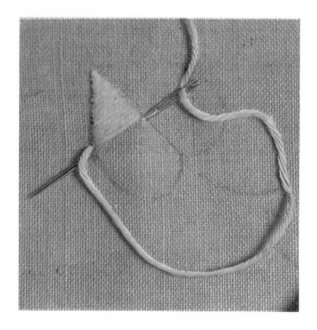

How to embroider
Satin stitch consists of vertical stitches placed side by side; begin from the lower left edge of the motif to be filled and re-insert the needle from top to bottom on each stitch. The only difficulty will be found in keeping the outline sharp and clear when the design presents irregular, curved motifs, or thin areas alternating with thick ones. When the motif is curved and the outer edge is larger than the inner edge, you must direct the

On the bottom of the preceding page: the movement of the needle in satin stitch to give a clear and regular contour. Top photo, same page: detail of tablecloth, shown on this page, revealing its unsophisticated and simple style.

In the picture below: in this breakfast cloth, the satin stitch seems to play with the little checks, inventing its own fanciful pattern. However, satin stitch is generally used on more ornate patterns.

stitches like a halo of rays, thickening them on the inner edge and spacing them on the outer edge. If the motif widens too much at any one point, causing the thread tension to loosen, you should divide the area into equal parts to be embroidered separately, and direct the stitches to meet at a center V point.

Yes to the embroidery frame

Although the frame is not strictly necessary for small areas or motifs, it will become irreplaceable on larger areas where the motif manifests a well defined shape requiring perfect thread tension and well distributed stitches. If possible, use a round frame.

THE PADDED SATIN STITCH

This adds a new dimension to the satin stitch, embellishing and emphasizing with a preliminary padding that underlines its total character. This ever-useful stitch can be employed on a multitude of things, all characterized by the same apparent simplicity.
Although similar in execution to the plain satin stitch, the effect is quite different (more elegant, richer). Used together they complement each other perfectly, giving great variety to any design.

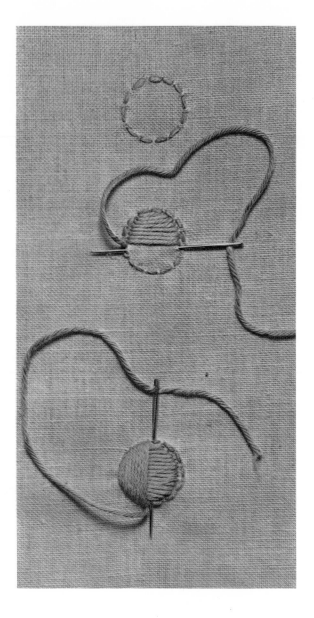

The design

The reproduction of the design for this stitch is no different than for others having the same characteristics. The final execution of the stitch depends largely upon the eye and the hand of the embroideress; a less than perfect execution will easily alter the outlines of a motif. Therefore, two identical pieces of work embroidered by different people will show a decided difference in personality.

The thread and the fabric

As in the case of the other satin stitch, this one also lends itself to any material and thread. However, the stitch manifests its best possibilities when used for delicate applications on light materials and small motifs.
This satin stitch is irreplaceable for embroidering initials, large flowery monograms and the fashionable 19th century style medallions used, in today's fashion, on the center fold of sheets or on corners of tablecloths. In these cases the preliminary padding is made with heavy thread; single ply mouliné thread is used over it for the final phase.

In the left photo: preparation of satin stitch applied to circles; first make a running stitch outline, then a thin satin stitch worked horizontally, then the final stitching to cover the motif. On the opposite page, right, a group of handkerchiefs with large initials.

How to embroider

The technique is the same as the previous stitch. Initial preparation is responsible for the difference in this stitch. You can proportion the padding of the motif to be embroidered to whatever texture you choose. After the preliminary running stitch outline, you may fill the center with other running stitches for light padding, or the horizontal satin stitches for deeper texture.

Always use the frame

Experience teaches us that satin stitch can only be perfectly executed when using the frame, regardless of whether or not it is handier without one. The round frame is best, of course, since it allows us to stretch the material exactly on the straight grain and consequently presents no problems.

The padded satin stitch on extremely small motifs is the most suitable for emphasizing the exquisite beauty of romantic initials so fashionable today. In these monograms, as in the ones on the previous page, the satin stitch creates a charming design, emphasized by pastel colors, blending perfectly with the background fabric of batiste. The same initials, on a larger scale, can be embroidered in the center fold of a sheet. (Guinetti-Milan)

THE ILLUSORY SHADOW STITCH

The quality of this stitch begins with its evocative yet literal name; it is considered part of sophisticated embroidery, although its technique seems rather elementary. Its secret is in the absolute clarity of its delicately executed contours, which only an expert hand can give it. The stitch gets its effect from the play of shadows and the illusion of transparency. It is a fragile stitch, best emphasized by organdy, linen-lawn and transparent fabrics which allow us to see its characteristic light shadows underneath.

Shadow stitch, in fact, acts on the wrong side of the work, showing a double back stitched outline on the right side which frames the recessed, shaded area. This stitch plays the main role in elegant dinner cloths which compliment the fine china, crystal and silver used upon them. It is also regal-looking when used on christening outfits. It is worthwhile to overcome any hesitancy in using this stitch in order to know the intimate pleasure of embroidering a luxurious tablecloth instead of purchasing a ready made one.

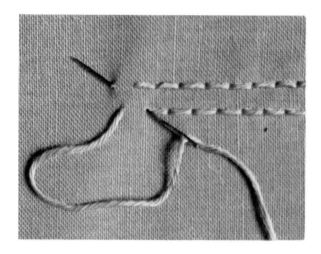 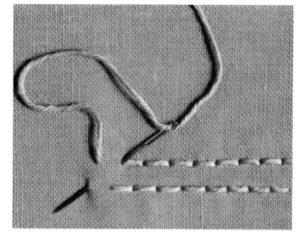

In the picture above left: the first phase of shadow stitch made with a frame. On the right: the second phase.

The design

Given the fragility of materials suited to shadow stitch, a light sure hand is essential in transferring the design. Carbon paper or, better still, a perforated pattern using powdered chalk, is used.

When using a frame, the design is drawn on the right side of the material, along with all motifs in which shadow stitch is combined with others, such as four-sided stitch, satin stitch, stem stitch, etc.

When you are not using the frame, the design is drawn, and the work is done, on the wrong side of the cloth. This is done only when the shadow stitch is used alone, for example, on sheets or tablecloths where large scalloped hems are worked with a shadow stitch.

The thread

One ply of the six-strand mouliné thread is most suitable; if you desire a more evident, yet functional outline, use a thin perle. Sometimes, on very fine fabrics, the thread is used to add color tone as well as to define the outline.

In this case, use pastel colors, which will give the embroidery a more beautiful effect when showing through the delicate transparency of the material.

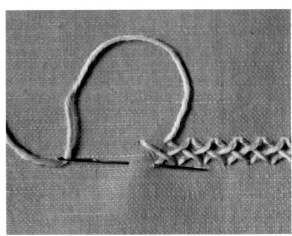

Shown left, top right and opposite: an impressive cloth in which the shadow stitch blends with others equally elegant.
Directly above: detail of execution of shadow stitch worked without a frame on the reverse of the material.

How to embroider shadow stitch

Theoretically, shadow stitch is very simple. It is made with a double back stitch worked very evenly, passing alternately from one side of the design to the other so that threads cross on the back of the fabric. One difficulty is presented when the design is enlarged or develops curves and circles; in this case, the outer stitches must be slightly larger than the inner stitches so that the threads on the back cross uniformly.

In this luxurious cloth, the geometric design of the shadow stitch makes it look like a woven fabric. Patience is needed to do the nets outlining the flowers which are also made with a shadow stitch. It is embroidered with a frame; a colored liner under the cloth will give the motifs the necessary prominence.

With a frame

Shadow stitch is worked in the opposite direction when using the frame; it is worked from right to left. Draw the needle out on the lower outline and insert it again in the fabric moving about four threads to the right. From the back of the work, the needle is drawn out again on the upper outline moving it towards the left; the needle then re-enters the fabric, after taking the usual four threads to the right and re-appears on the lower outline to the left. Although the description of the method sounds complicated, it is relatively easy to do. The execution of shadow stitch with a frame permits a view of the entire work and therefore results in greater precision in the length and alignment of stitches.

Without a frame

Draw the design on the back of the fabric and work from left to right. After drawing the needle out on the left below the design, move diagonally towards the upper outline and take up about four threads from right to left. Return diagonally towards the right on the lower outline, make a stitch from left to right identical to the previous one and continue, taking care to cross at regular intervals. In order to control the crossing of this herringbone stitch, shadow stitch is easier to do by hand than with a frame.

PAINTING WITH THE LONG AND SHORT FILLING STITCH

This is one of the classical embroidery stitches suitable for the individual with a great deal of patience and time at her disposal; it is a noble and important stitch used to paint colored and shaded motifs with the diligence and enthusiasm of a realistic painter. This stitch requires self-assurance as it does not allow for hesitation and eventual regrets; it demands a firm hand and a sure sense of color. Each stitch lines up next to the previous one, at the same time shaping out the motif on which it operates. Its characteristics are especially emphasized when embroidered on lightweight fabrics such as sheer linen weaves, batiste, or organdy; it prefers motifs with flowers, particularly roses, where the position of the petals and shading of colors must be emphasized.

The design

The design must be lightly drawn but clearly visible; the carbon paper method, used with care, is advisable. Keep a light hand, make clear outlines, but keep them light, as a heavy line will show through even after embroidering.

The thread

Mouliné thread is classic for this filling stitch, as it gives the surface of the work that smooth and moderately shiny appearance that entitles it to the additional qualification of a paint stitch. Use only one ply, especially when using the shaded type. Nevertheless, it is more exciting to create the shades ourselves; use lighter shades at the outer edges of the motif and increase the depth of color as you work towards the center. To embroider heavy silks or faille (there are still some people who cherish them), use a silken thread, in even paler colors, with a controlled sheen.

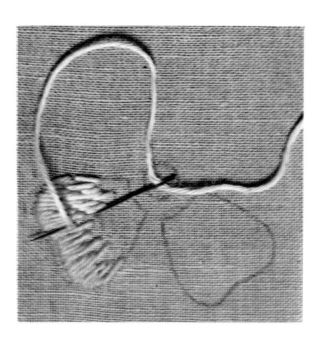

The left to right movement of the needle places rows of irregular short and long filling stitches, one after the other.

How to embroider it

The technique of this stitch is very similar to satin stitch; it is made by lining up vertical stitches, inserting the needle from top to bottom and moving from left to right.

However, the stitch does not fill the entire surface of the motif immediately, but advances with long and short stitches. It is the embroideress' job to use her talent and sense of improvisation to align the rows of stitches to best advantage, as they are never drawn on the cloth. The first row follows the outer edge of the motif, leaving the inner edge with irregular stitches. The second row is the

Above: the short and long filling stitch on this set of doilies is frail, almost transparent, made on lightest weight linen using one ply mouliné thread. The enlarged detail, to the left, reveals the absence of other stitches; the short and long filling stitch is sufficient for this simple, but tasteful motif.

In the large picture opposite: on the edge of this scalloped bed sheet, a rose in the classical paint stitch with shaded rows that emphasize its colors and blossoms. Below, this page, a detail showing the shaded color from pale pink to deepest pink.

hardest; it also starts from the left and the stitches are placed in alternating lengths, (short stitches below long ones and vice versa).

You must always estimate the number of rows necessary to fill the entire pattern so that stitches do not overlap. Careful calculation will result in a smooth surface with a water color effect.

The frame is helpful

The round frame lends valuable assistance to this embroidery as it keeps the material taut and the stitches become more pronounced. It will also facilitate the calculation of each row and enable you to slant the stitches directly towards the center. Always begin with the outer row of stitches.

THERE IS ALSO
THE CHINESE FILLING STITCH

It is pleasant to think of a filling stitch named Chinese as symbolic of a people who love the complicated but face it with extreme lucidity and calm. In fact, this is a simplified version of the short and long filling stitch; halfway between it and the satin stitch. In this version, the zones of color are put together in distinct rows instead of being shaded together. The effect is just as pretty and also reminds us of a painting, not quite as realistic, but still very efficacious and original. The truly Chinese versions are very colorful; however, our taste gives preference to the light shades that repeat those of the classic filling stitch in a different effect.

The material and the thread

Material and thread correspond to those of the traditional filling stitch, with perhaps slight preference given to finer threads that thicken and give a block appearance to the color when embroidered. The reproduction also presents no problems and you may use any of the three classical methods.

How to embroider

For the Chinese filling stitch, the motif to be filled must have been previously divided into two or more areas, each one representing a color. Once

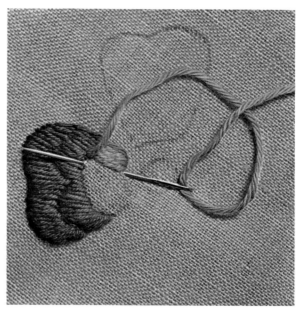

In the picture on the right, the movement of the needle in the Chinese filling stitch. Contrary to the classic one, the Chinese filling stitch requires the darker shades at the outer limits of the motif, obtaining a reverse effect to the traditional one.
Above: a detail of the hand towels on the next page.

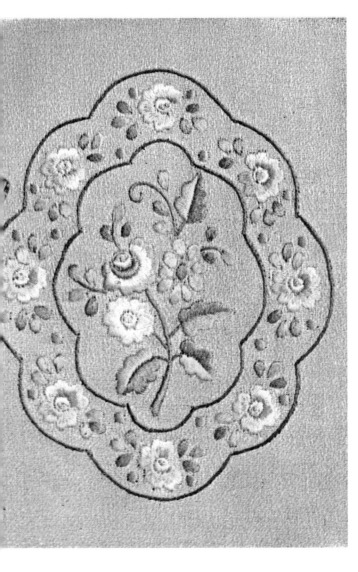

with a padding of running stitches similar to the crossing stitches used on satin stitch.

Use the frame

The use of the frame for the chinese filling stitch is of utmost importance in maintaining perfect thread tension, perfect alignment of the rows and to direct the halo shaping towards the center. The round frame is more suitable because it is handier and more precise.

On the right: the Chinese filling stitch and the classic one are embroidered on these liberty-style garlands which are perfect for guest towels; all in pastel colors.
On the left, above: details of a motif surrounded by the stem stitch.

the work is finished it will have a heavy texture, so each area will have to look plausible and comply with the general design of the motif as well as bringing out the colors. Obviously, not every motif can be divided into sections; you will therefore have to choose clear motifs, well separated from each other.

Each area is worked in satin stitch, starting from the outer edges, and care must be taken to keep the outlines very clean; the colored zones must remain distinct even though close together. Absolute perfection may be obtained by preparing each area

THE PARMA STITCH IS ALTOGETHER ENJOYABLE

Parma stitch is sumptuous, almost baroque in appearance, yet has a very modern and rather contained elegance. It imitates manufactured ribbon braid with unsurpassed delicacy and versatility; in fact, even when circling in tight spirals, where commercial braid would lie flat, Parma stitch develops a solid, light grace on a dynamic and perfectly developed background.

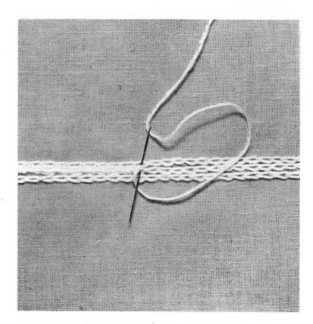

First stage of Parma stitch.

The thread and the material

This stitch shows to best advantage when done in white or off-white heavy cotton or wool, or the heaviest perlé, on very dark or very bright colors. The best basic material is always a heavy linen or linen-hemp mixture. After a long, undeserved period of disuse, Parma stitch has been re-discovered in this new, modern white on bright look.

The design

Quiet, solid, good natured Parma stitch accepts any type of design. The only specific requirement is that the two parallel lines forming the foundation must follow a regular course with a fixed distance of 1/2 inch between them. Draw one exact portion

of the design and keep reproducing it along the entire course in order to maintain perfect regularity.

How to embroider it

Parma stitch is a combination of the chain and blanket stitch, but it is as amusing and absorbing as a game. Start with a base made of three rows of chain stitch; the first row on the upper outline, second row in the middle and third row on the lower outline. It is important to remember that

Second stage of Parma stitch.

all three rows must follow the same direction and each stitch must be the same length. Naturally, on curves the outer row will have to have slightly longer stitches than the inner row in order to maintain the same number of stitches.

You can now begin the additional texture which is formed by two rows of the blanket stitch. The first row is worked on the second and third of the six threads of the chain; the second row is worked on the fourth and fifth threads. Be very careful to keep the needle from picking up any threads of the fabric on these two rows. Two or three blanket stitches are made in each chain (depending on the length of the chains); work from left to right in a direction that places the blanket knot in the center of the work. The second row is worked in the same way so that knots of each row meet in the center, leaving the first and sixth thread of the chain free to give lightness and grace to the contours of the finished work.

In the picture below: the chalk-white curves on a bright blue background underline the braid-like Parma embroidery that proceeds with a rapid but accurate rhythm. To the right, a detail.

Use two needles

To ease the passage of the needle under the two loops of the chain stitch without catching the fabric underneath, you have the choice of two methods. Either use an embroidery needle for the chain stitch and a tapestry needle for the blanket stitch, or use the embroidery needle only and during the second stage of the work pass the thread through with the eye end.

THE NOBILITY OF FLORENTINE TRAPUNTO

We could almost call this a heavier version of the shadow stitch. In fact, just as in shadow stitch, this is formed by a double line of almost parallel stitches surrounding a shaded zone. Florentine trapunto has a rather deep texture, created with thick wool inserted through the back of the work which delicately colors and stuffs the relief.

This is an old decorating technique which originated in Florence, Italy yet is extremely modern in style because it is neither too pompous nor over-embroidered. Even though fashion alternately accepts and rejects this type of quilting, its application to organdy, light silk spreads, and crib covers remains eternal for softness, lightness, and elegance.

Gofffré is another, less elegant, but more practical type of quilting which can be made with a sewing machine and has been widely used and adopted for quilted material sold in yard goods departments.

The design

Florentine trapunto requires a very light design. As a matter of fact, even if it is drawn on the back of the work, the sheerness of the fabrics used, plus

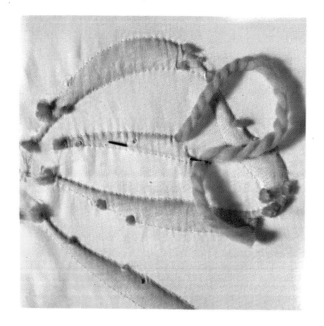

the fact that the running stitch conceals very little, is reason enough to try to prevent the design from showing on the right side. It is, therefore, best to use the perforated pattern method.

Not all designs are suitable for the Florentine stitch; they must have a definite course, an almost geometrical shape and avoid too large or too rounded forms in which the yarn could bunch up, creating an ugly protuberance.

The material and thread

The most authentic version of Florentine trapunto calls for a semi-transparent material, such as silk or organdy, for the right side of the work, placed over another stronger, but soft, opaque material like a cotton muslin for the lining. If you wish the quilting motif only, without color filtering through the surface layer, both fabrics can be opaque and heavy, to give a padded texture.

For the Goffré quilt, the fabric choice is wider and includes woolens, cottons and even printed materials.

How to embroider it

The outlines of Florentine quilting are made with short, thick running stitches. Put the two layers of material together with some scattered basting; transfer the chosen design on the wrong side and outline its contours with brief and regular running stitches. Thread a thick, blunt point wool needle with thick wool and pad the motifs by passing it between the layers, through the double lines on the back of the work. If the design has a geometric regularity, threading the wool through the motif once or twice is sufficient. If the design contains areas which widen, then narrow, it is necessary to do additional padding. Re-thread the areas requiring thicker padding as many times as is necessary to maintain the same over-all texture.

Everything is easier on the Goffré quilt. Place a third layer of cotton batting between the top layer and lining; tack the layers together and proceed with a running stitch through the layers. For a firmer quilting, use the back stitch and trace the design on the right side of the work.

Note: The grain of the fabrics layered together must always run in the same direction.

On the opposite page: the wrong side of the work in Florentine trapunto. The various points where the needle entered are clearly visible and well marked by wisps of wool which must not be cut, but left slightly protruding, so that the padding will retain its shape perfectly. Below: a favorite motif for Florentine trapunto; very suitable for organdy crib covers.

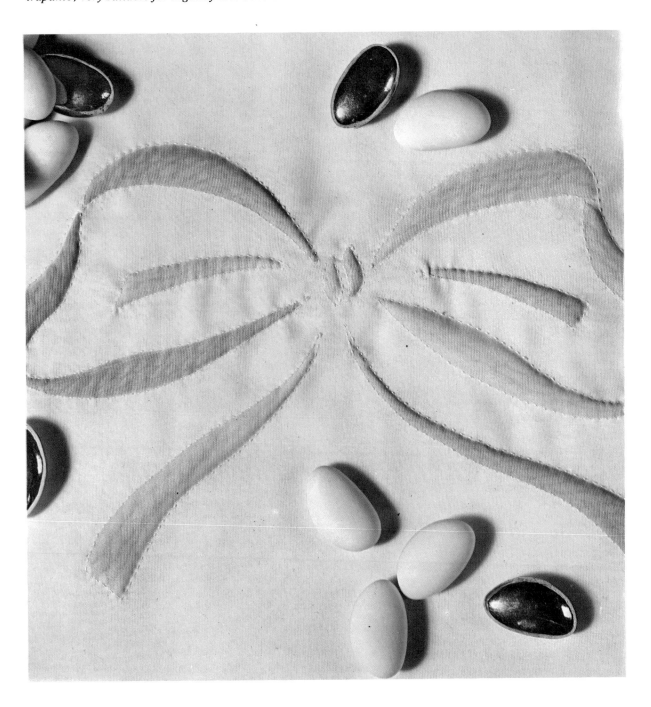

SLIP STITCH HAS NO HISTORY

This stitch has neither tradition nor high ancestry; it is a newcomer to the group of filling stitches. After stealing ideas here and there, a little from stem stitch, a little from satin stitch and even running stitch, it has developed a style of its own, and does a fine job as a filling stitch. This almost unknown stitch bursts upon the scene in radiant colors to fill the appealing and simple motifs that are favorites in modern embroidery.

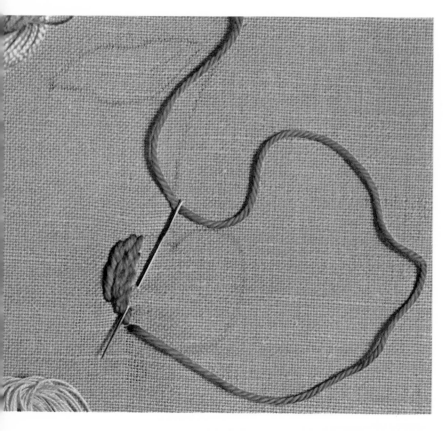

In the picture above: in order to emerge at 1/3 the length of the preceding stitch, the needle enters the fabric slightly diagonally in slip stitch. On the large picture: a delightfully colorful place mat.

The material and thread

This is a stitch born of color, under the sign of simplicity; it never betrays these characteristics even in the choice of material and thread, which are usually easy and bright. The opaque but clearly colored woolen thread is best suited to create little islands of color on a background of heavy linen or hemp. If it is embroidered color over color with cotton or mouliné the slip stitch does itself proud and holds its own with filling stitches like bokhara couching.

How to embroider it

This stitch allows total freedom for personal interpretation in its execution. The final effect is always the same, neither a running stitch nor a short and long filling stitch. Start at the lower left and move to the top of the work in the same manner as the stem stitch. The needle is inserted from top to bottom, each time emerging at 1/3 the length of the previous stitch. When reaching the top outline of the motif, you may either turn the work and start again, (the previously embroidered row will now be on the right and the stitch will shade slightly lighter) or return the needle to the lower edge on the wrong side of the work and continue in the same direction as the first row.

In the most authentic version of the slip stitch, the needle splits the thread of the previous stitch in half when emerging at the 1/3 point.

The design

The slip stitch is another one which presents no problems when using the regular carbon paper transfer method. One very good suggestion for a design utilizing this stitch is the stylized fruit on the place mat pictured on the preceding page. For your convenience, we have illustrated them here in their actual size. You may take advantage of this by tracing the fruit onto a piece of transparent paper and making your own transfer design.

In the three pictures: details of the place mat on preceding page in their actual sizes. It is the commonplace fruit seen in a naive, but very ornamental way, that offers a multitude of ideas for different applications.

BRODERIE ANGLAISE
IS BACK IN STYLE

The prevailing taste for antiques and old things has returned to Broderie Anglaise or eyelet work to prominence. This is a gay and pretty stitch that has supported a century of tradition in white embroidery, survived the ever changing trends of fashion, and today retains its rightful place in the group of most popular stitches. Perhaps its success is due to the designs it prefers: small, unsophisticated cut-out shapes of leaves and daisies, or scattered eyelets that once were always present on linen curtains, tablecloths and bedspreads. Even today, the 19th century style of Broderie Anglaise maintains a following of its own that periodically and successfully returns it to current fashion.

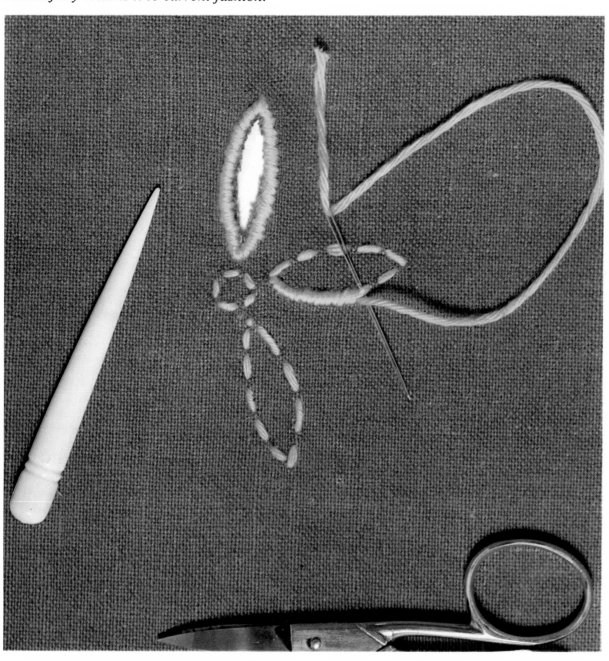

The design

Design reproduction for the Broderie Anglaise is uncomplicated. Since the motifs always have small dimensions and the leaves and eyelets which compose them must never vary, it is advisable to use the perforated pattern method which provides a more exact reproduction than the carbon paper method.

The material and thread

Linen fabric and white perlé thread for embroidering are always most appropriate as they can withstand the heavy ironing necessary to enhance the stitching in classical Broderie Anglaise.

The finished embroidery must be ironed on the wrong side, over a soft cloth, to maintain the contour of the stitches and prevent them from being

On page 65 the simplest version of Broderie Anglaise with its indispensable accessories; scissors and bodkin. On this page on the left: the discreet grace of Broderie Anglaise also adapts to applications that contradict it, as in the case of the rough material and unromantic color of this tablecloth. Above: an enlarged detail.

flattened by the iron. Iron in one direction only, following the straight fabric grain and avoiding circular movements. A bodkin, inserted from the wrong side towards the right, will return the eyelet to a perfectly round shape.

How to embroider

There are two versions of Broderie Anglaise, each giving an almost identical final effect. One, more simplified and suitable for many motifs, requires

a preliminary running stitch on the outline of the little leaf, followed by a thick cording. After finishing the embroidery, the fabric inside the motif is cut away on the wrong side, close to the cording, with a sharp, bent scissors.

In the classical version of Broderie Anglaise, the excess material is cut while embroidering. After the preliminary running stitch, the material inside the leaf is slashed in the length and folded under to each side as you embroider, giving the cording additional padding.

In the case of a large leaf, cut a long oval out of the center, leaving a thin edge near the outline and fold this under into the cording while embroidering. If the motif is an eyelet, pierce the fabric in the center with a bodkin and widen the hole to the desired degree with a steady, circular pressure.

Note: the excess material must be completely covered by the cording so that no trace of the folded material is visible even on the wrong side.

POLITICS AND HIGH FINANCE CREATED
THE RICHELIEU STITCH (CUTWORK)

Everyone is aware that fashion is primarily an economic factor that can change in a moment into an esthetic tradition. The propagation of the Richelieu stitch began in the 17th century, in the year 1635, when the great statesman issued a drastic edict. In order to decrease the quantity of valuable currency going abroad, he decided to place limitations on lace imported from Italy and Belgium, and to manufacture a typically French lace creation. This lace was named d'Alençon after the town in which the factory was established.

With the intention of creating a market for Alençon, he started the lace madness which kept all the nobles and wealthy people of that time under cascades of lace.

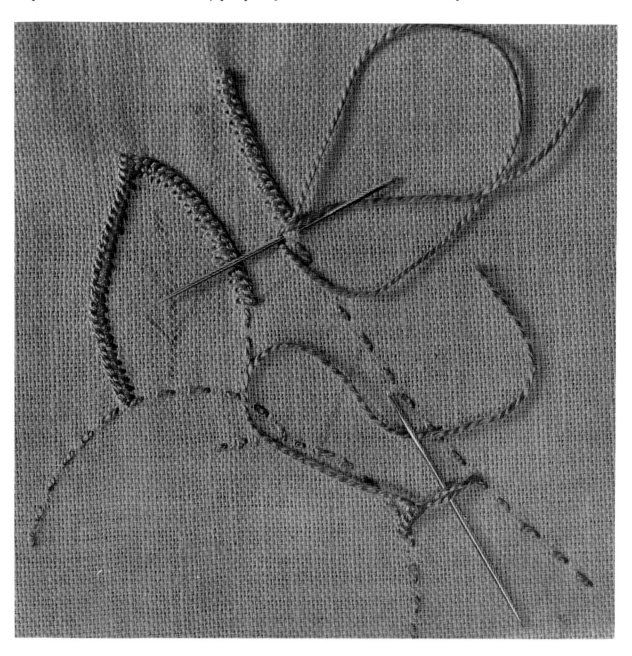

Since then this stitch, bearing its creator's name, has undergone several simplifications that gradually changed it from the stiff, original version into the lighter and more approachable one. Today, after periods of ups and downs, cutwork of both the Richelieu and lighter guipure types have returned to a place of honor in modern homes where it creates a polished contrast to twentieth century styling.

The material and thread

Always use stark white for both fabric and thread and you will have an excellent start toward ultimate elegance. The fabric must be firm enough to support the weight of the embroidery and withstand the pressure of heavy ironing necessary in laundering. Cotton materials and heavy linen are suitable and the thread must be twisted and heavy; in this case use the perle or cotton.

The design

It is not easy to find authentic designs which can be reproduced in a simplified, yet modern, manner. At any rate, once your search has been successful, the design must be reproduced with extreme clarity using either carbon paper or the perforated pattern method.

Richelieu or not?

Richelieu stitch can be carried out by using different stitches to remedy its heaviness and lighten it to more modern proportions, yet still maintain its general characteristics. The original Richelieu stitch, immortalized in portraits of dames and cardinals by painters like Rubens or Van Dyck, has padded motifs covered with satin stitch, attached to one another by little bars and picots that make the work too rigid and heavy. When we eliminate the picots, retain the bars, and use the blanket stitch or cording without padding on the outlines, the stitch is called guipure.

At cocktail time, the little cloth embroidered with guipure is a markedly new idea destined for success, as it blends with every decor. The design must be antique though, in order to exalt its lightness and grace. The same stitch may be used on curtains and luxurious tablecloths. On page 67, the movement of the needle in Richelieu stitch.

The picots which are embroidered on the authentic Richelieu stitch are worked as follows: when reaching the center of the bar, wrap the thread around the needle eight times and re-enter at the same point where the needle emerged. A small loop gathered around the center hole will be formed when the needle is pulled gently through this wrapping; finish the other half bar.

The heavier areas to be embroidered with the satin stitch require a preparation similar to that used for the classical satin stitch, either close, thick running stitches or a padding of crossing satin stitches.

When the embroidery is all finished, detach the waxed paper and trim away all the excess material between motifs; use a sharp bent scissors on the wrong side. Don't forget to be extremely cautious when cutting; work slowly and carefully!

Above: a detail of the elegant cloth shown on the previous page. It is entirely blanket stitch with bars, but without picots. On the right: the most recent and even lighter version of guipure. It is all cording, with a hint of slip stitch, on stark white pillowcases.

How to embroider

The embroidery is first basted, one area at a time, to a special waxed paper which is available in all needlework shops. This keeps the fabric well distributed and, at the same time, retains its manageability. The stitches of cutwork are anti-frame like blanket stitch and cording. Baste thickly, following the course of the design, keeping 1/4 inch inside the motifs.

The base is a running stitch, placed exactly over the outline of the drawing; when reaching a bar, form a little bridge with two long stitches, placed exactly over the outline, and cover these two threads with a buttonhole stitch (without catching the fabric with the needle). When you have finished a bar, start the running stitch along the outline again until you reach the next bar and repeat the procedure. When all the bars have been completed, the contours of the motifs are then embroidered in one continuous movement.

THE TURKISH STITCH AND FOUR-SIDED STITCH ARE BRILLIANT AND CONSTRUCTIVE

The four-sided stitch and Turkish stitch deserve a separate discussion, as they are the independents in the family of stitches, built on a mosaic of objectives and destinations. Each one requires drawn threads on compact material, but can manage well on thin material having a clearly visible warp and woof, or, in the case of Turkish stitch, if the course is irregular.

The four-sided stitch is a specialty of plain tablecloths and is used on miles and miles of napkin and tablecloth hems whether embroidered or not. The Turkish stitch, once popular in the hand-made, silken underwear field, is now seen only in lavish movies of the thirties. Nevertheless, it still maintains a privileged position and is used to affix hems or laces on fine tablecloths, and occasionally on some appliqué work.

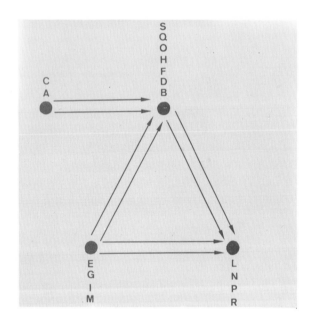

row at which point the next stitch will start.

After a few motifs the stitch becomes logical and automatic. The little sketch of the course of the needle will be very helpful, and with a reasonable amount of practice you will be able to work quickly.

On the left: the course of the Turkish stitch. Below: the course of the four-sided stitch depicted clearly and concisely in alphabetical order, assisted by unmistakable directional arrows.

How to embroider four-sided stitch

A basic preparation is always necessary; it consists of drawing two threads out of the material, leaving four threads intact between the drawn rows.

Working from right to left, draw the needle out on the lower row of drawn threads. Take a vertical stitch into the upper row, passing the needle on the wrong side and bringing it out four threads to the left on the lower row. It then moves to the right and returns again to the base of the vertical stitch, forming a horizontal stitch. The needle then passes diagonally on the wrong side and emerges four threads to the left on the upper row. It completes a horizontal stitch on the right, passes diagonally under the fabric and emerges on the lower

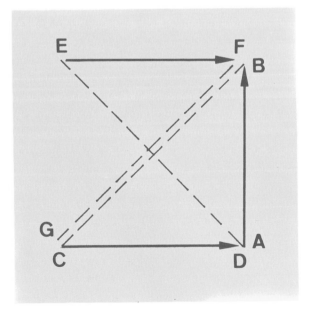

How to embroider Turkish stitch

This stitch takes a lot of running-in, which is accomplished by carefully and steadily following the various stages drawn on the sketch. In a short time you will be pleasantly surprised to realize that the movement is spontaneous, almost mechanical, and runs smoothly without other guides.

Turkish stitch advances from left to right with a series of parallel and alternate stitches joined together by oblique stitches; each movement is repeated twice. If the stitch is to be embroidered on the straight thread, it is helpful and more comfortable to draw two threads and leave four threads in between.

In the picture below: on the orange material, Turkish stitch advancing from left to right without considering the grain of the fabric. On the blue material: the four-sided stitch which demands the strictest straight grain and advances from right to left.

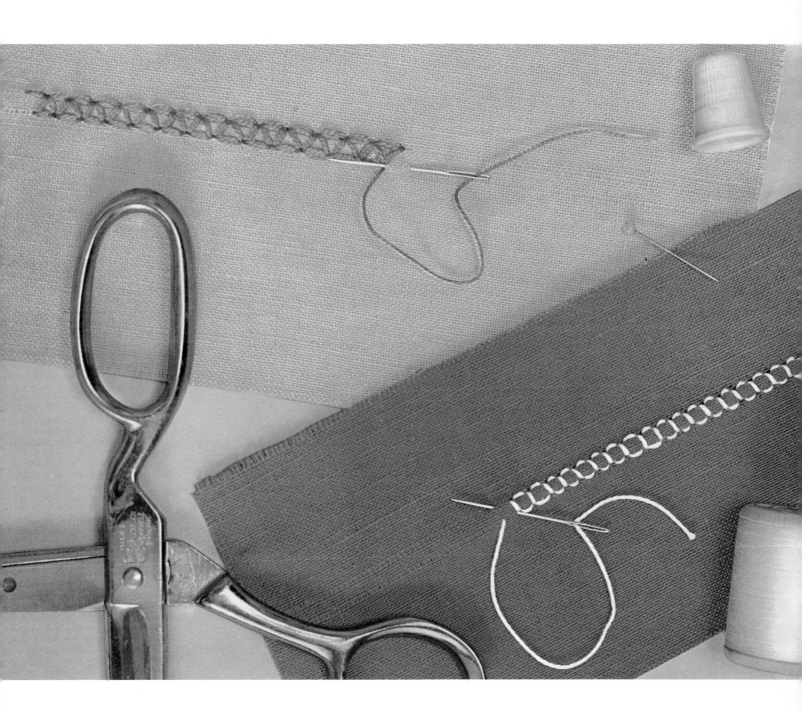

ECHOES OF THE 19TH CENTURY IN HEMSTITCHING

This is a vast group of stitches, rich in the traditions of a vague, Victorian era. Today, fashion has turned its back on the majority of them, considering them impractical, for no one can deny the laundering problems they present. Yet it defers to the simple hemstitch, ladder hemstitch and the more complicated, but decorative, Fleur-de-lis, to provide that finished touch to all household linen. It is used on tablecloths of many types, sheets, pillowcases, and even lends a grace and refinement to summer dresses.

The material and preparation

Obviously, designs for drawn thread works are non-existent; it is the duty of the fabric, with its well visible warp and woof, to guide the rhythm of the stitch. Draw a number of threads from the fabric to correspond to the desired border width and then fasten the threads differently in various groups. (See stitching instructions.) The thread is to be adjusted from time to time to the firmness of the material on which it is being worked.

After establishing the width of the border, you must consider the thickness of the threads, not the quantity. For example: for a 1/2 inch drawn thread border, 8 threads of a medium weight fabric might be sufficient, while a lighter fabric would require a greater number. Always measure while drawing the threads. Drawing threads should be done very carefully. Since drawn threads must conform to the shape of a corner, they must stop at a certain point and then be drawn on the perpendicular to define a straight angle. In this case, it is necessary to establish the exact point of the angle and draw from there in both directions. This must be done in order to leave the corner material intact.

Simple hemstitch

This is the universal method used to affix hems on all household linen, tablecloths and handkerchiefs included. First determine the width of the hem you are supposed to fold and tack, and then proceed to draw the threads above this line.

Working from left to right, fasten the thread under the hem, take a fixed number of threads (3 to 5), passing the needle under the drawn threads from

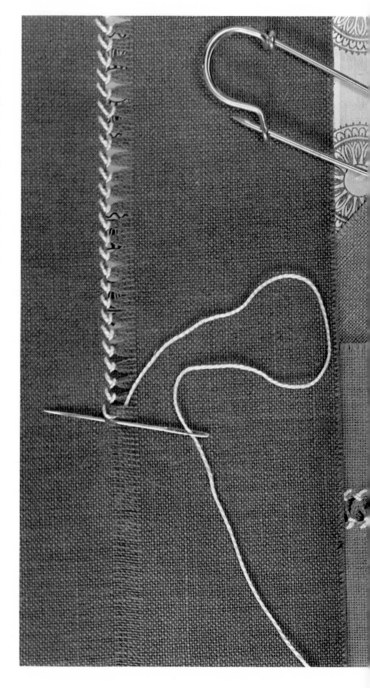

right to left, and draw the needle out. After this, take two threads from the fold of the hem, another portion of the drawn threads, and continue in this manner to the end.

Simple hemstitch on the brown fabric; ladder hemstitch on the purple; a sample of serpentine hemstitch on the blue.

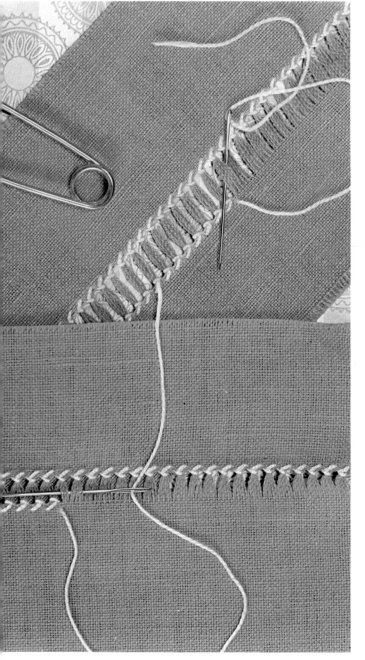

Ladder hemstitch

Work the same as the previous stitch but on each side of the drawn threads, creating a series of vertical groupings. In the upper row, where the hem is missing, the vertical stitch is made on the material in between the groupings.

Saw tooth or serpentine hemstitch

This is a very nice, also practical stitch, still used quite often as a light and simple decoration on sheets and pillowcases. Its ideal setting is on borders; two rows of serpentine hemstitch are placed about 3 inches apart and a row of satin stitch dots between. When working serpentine hemstitch, the groupings must have an even number of threads as the second row combines one half of each of two adjacent groupings into one, thus forming the serpentine line..

ELABORATE HEMSTITCHES

The easy and fascinating rhythm of the basic hemstitch becomes almost hypnotic after awhile. The traditional embroidery presents an endless variety of crossings and knottings, some of them so elaborate that they become taboo in our modern concept. A few manage to survive and they are the ones to which fashion returns periodically, featuring them on summer dresses as fresh and elegant insertions.

Knotting of groups of threads

These are generally grouped in sets of three. First prepare the border with the usual groupings (a larger number of threads will emphasize the effect). Working from right to left, wrap the thread around the center of three groupings. After fastening the threads on the right, wrap it around the next 3 groupings, then pass the needle under the grouping, inside the loop of thread, and pull gently to form a knot from which you skip to the next one and repeat the procedure.

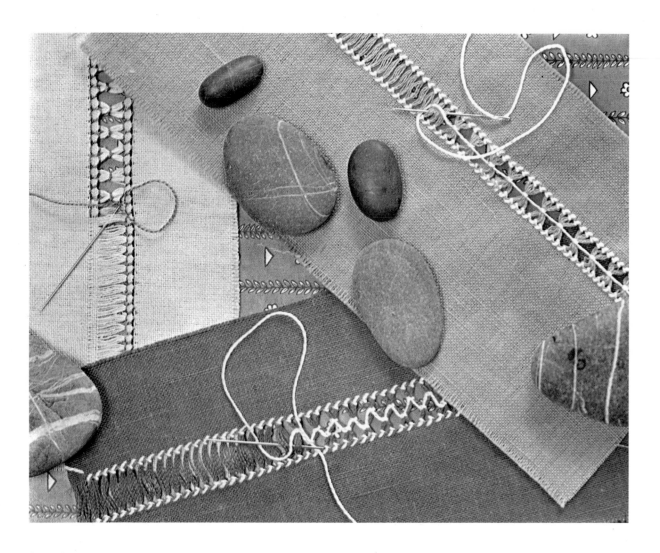

Interlacing groups of threads

In this particular system of knotting, the thread does not skip from one group to another, but passes under the work creating an additional ornamental effect. Work from right to left. Notice that the method of wrapping the thread creates a difference between the top and bottom knot. In the upper knot, the thread is the same as in knotting groups of thread: it forms a loop on the left, then is knotted by the needle passing under the groupings and inside the thread loop. When the thread is passed down along the grouping in the direction of the knot below, the needle enters the loop of thread with an upward movement instead of a downward one.

Fleur-de-lis

The fleur-de-lis is ornamental and meticulous on sheets and pillowcases, original and youthful in a

On the pink material: knotting of groups of threads. On the blue: interlacing groups of threads. On the white: a fleur-de-lis. All three methods of grouping work from right to left.

gigantic size on summer dresses. It requires a more complicated preparation for drawing the threads: draw one thread, skip four threads, draw six or eight threads, skip four threads and draw one more. First, make a row of simple four-sided stitch along the lower edge of the drawn threads. Then, begin the second row of four-sided stitch along the upper edge, tying the groupings together in pairs as follows: work from right to left, taking care to line the stitches up with the first row, and allow the thread to descend to the center of a grouping, tying it to the next group with the usual looped knot, then return to the upper row and begin the next four-sided stitch.

RODI STITCH:
OPENWORK EMBROIDERY

The distinguished, personalized rodi stitch, along with all the other filling stitches, introduces a trend of new ideas expressed with the light and fascinating art of the most precious laces. It usually flourishes in scattered motifs on thin material, true islands of beauty that highlight the other stitches combined with the rodi stitch. Sometimes there is a mistaken belief that filling stitches are reserved only for professional embroideresses; but, if it is faced with patience and an explanatory sketch showing the movements of the needle, even the pulled fabric stitches are easily accomplished and diverting. Their rhythmic movement, guided by the web of the fabric, provides that irreplaceable relaxation so often thought to be the exclusive prerogative of canvas stitches.

The fabric and the thread

With an admirable ambivalence, rodi stitch keeps its light and precise effect—whether in elegant motifs on thin materials when combined with short and long filling stitch and shadow stitch, or on rather firm materials with enlarged dimensions. Nothing detracts from its characteristic rhythm and elegance.

The thread is almost always one strand of mouline; either white on pastel fabrics, or matched color on colored fabrics, becoming almost invisible on the finished work. When the material is thick, a rather thick size of the white perle is advisable.

The design

Rodi stitch does not have a design per se, only a definite outline which is covered with a cording while working. This serves to underline the shape that has been filled with rodi stitch and to hide the inevitable irregularities that often show near the outer edges. When the basic threads under rodi stitch are drawn, the cording also helps in fastening the threads and strengthening their ends.

In the photo on the left: the movement of the needle in rodi stitch. The solid lines with arrows indicate the visible course and direction of the thread, while the broken lines indicate the course on the wrong side.

How to embroider

Rodi stitch, with drawn threads or without, proceeds along the fabric by counting threads accurately. It starts from the top right of the motif and proceeds diagonally toward the lower left for the return row. You must turn the work and repeat the same movement until the entire surface has been filled. The diagram on page 75 indicates the path of the needle proceeding towards the lower left and diagonally underneath. The needle emerges from the fabric at point A, re-enters four threads over to the right; moves diagonally under the fabric and emerges at point C four threads below A; it then comes up to point D, moves diagonally under the fabric and re-appears at point E, repeating the same movement over and over.

This technique produces a thick embroidery when the thread maintains normal tension; a perforated one if the thread is pulled taut. If you wish to give the work a more open look, you must prepare the basic drawn threads by pulling out a thread at predetermined fixed intervals, both from the warp and the woof.

Definitely use the frame!

The resourceful frame is indispensable, both for drawing the threads and working the stitch. In fact, it facilitates the work when the surface is fixed and taut. Draw one thread at a time, cutting off pieces with a sharp scissors, and removing it slowly without ever pulling on it. In this way, you will avoid tangling the remaining threads, which would be a catastrophe.

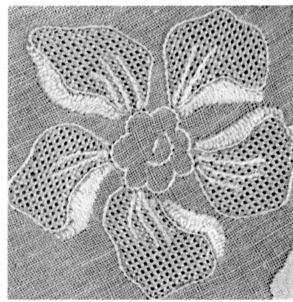

Illustration on the previous page shown here in detail. It is one of the most successful combinations: rodi stitch, short and long filling stitch, and shadow stitch combined on a tablecloth. On the left: rodi stitch in its lightest version, which successfully imitates lace.

PRINCESS OR OCTAGONAL FILLING STITCH

We are now going to show you another stitch with approximately the same characteristics as rodi stitch. Princess stitch follows a more complicated course as it traces very concise, attractive diagonals on the fabric. It is also applied to scattered motifs, competing with rodi stitch in delicacy and finesse; at times they are combined with elaborate elegance.
Princess stitch is successfully used, in its enlarged design, as a unique decoration on tablecloths of graceful simplicity. Thus, in harmony with its stylized elegance, this stitch develops a new dimension of embroidery, projecting its symmetry into a giant size.

The fabric and thread

Whether or not it is used in combination with rodi stitch, princess stitch demands the same light-weight fabrics, mainly important tablecloth linens, accompanied by mouline thread in matching color. In the more modern giant version, it is most effective on heavy linen or hopsack with twisted perle thread in white on pastel colors.

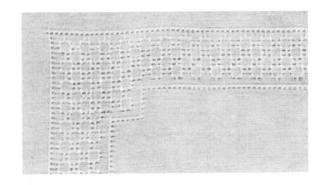

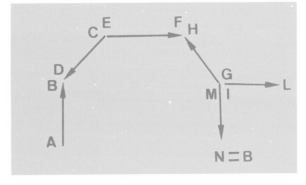

In the top photo: a detail of the pink tablecloth on page 78. Lower photo: the course of the needle in princess stitch.

The design and the frame

A design is unnecessary for princess stitch; you don't even have to draw threads. The only requirement is a strict counting of stitches that precludes any distractions or irregularities. The use of a frame is strongly advised as it will become indispensable when the stitch is executed in its enlarged version. Obviously, the frame should be large and square with a wide surface. When used for small motifs like rodi stitch, it is surrounded by a cording; if it is a large sized embroidery, like a whole border, it is always underlined on the sides by a four-sided stitch or hemstitch to point out its geometric character.

How to embroider

Princess stitch always proceeds in the same way, from left to right, lining up a series of half octagons which are completed on the second row after turning the work. The course of the needle is explained in the diagram above. The needle emerges from the fabric at point A, enters four threads farther on at point B, reappears at point C (four threads above and four threads to the right), disappears at point D, appears again at point E, and disappears again

four threads farther over at point F. The letters F to N represent the same course in the second row to complete the octagons. In repeating the course on following rows, point A-B is eliminated and the stitch begins from B. Naturally, after the initial difficulty of setting the pattern on the first row, the following rows will take an easier course as the new stitches are built on those of the preceding one.

THE STAR STITCH:
A FILLING STITCH OVER DRAWN THREADS

This is a dynamic stitch that happily concludes our adventure among the drawn thread works, to which we shall give the generic name of star stitch. Yet, the fact that it does not possess a specific name in no way removes the qualification of "easy and enjoyable" that accompanies it. Furthermore, it is a truly effective stitch which displays a comforting precision and security of hand on the very first attempt.

The fabric and thread

The material should be lightweight, with a thick and clearly visible weave. The thread should be obvious and always white so that it will be greatly emphasized by the colors of the background fabric. It is advisable to use a thickly woven linen or hand woven hemp and embroider with the thickest perle.

Use the frame

The only complicated operation of the star stitch is drawing the threads. Withdraw rows of four parallel threads, leaving four in between, in both

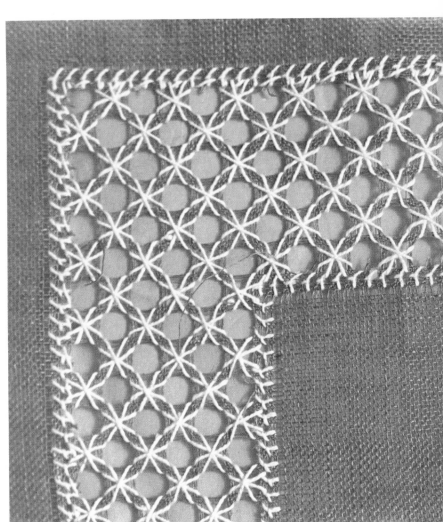

In the picture below: the course of the needle in star stitch. The same movement is repeated in all directions, with a right to left movement and return. On the right: a detail of the cloth on page 80, embroidered with a star filling stitch in its giant size, using white thread on a strawberry colored background of thickly woven linen.

a vertical and horizontal direction until you obtain an openwork net which is used as a base for the stitch. It is interesting to note that the material is to be put on the frame before withdrawing the threads, row by row. The basic net must be as clean as if it were manufactured that way, in order to insure a successful job. Obviously, when the tablecloth is wider than the frame, both withdrawing threads and embroidering must be done one section at a time, moving the frame as necessary.

How to embroider

The stitch is worked diagonally in two-way rows. Fasten the thread on the upper right of the work, proceed towards the lower left, passing the needle under each crossing of threads with a right to left movement. The return course uses the same technique in an opposite direction, thereby placing a series of parallel long X's on the fabric. When all the material has been filled in this manner, turn the work and repeat the same thing. When working the final row, finish the star by stopping in the center of each and taking a small stitch to fasten the crossed threads.

The star stitch filling in over drawn threads looks truly splendid on this tablecloth and its movement appears rapid and concise. The threads were drawn while the cloth was stretched on a slate frame.

APPLIQUÉ WORK
FOR FORM AND COLOR

Appliqué work is a winning combination of color, form, speed and rewarding effects. In fact, momentarily abandoning the proliferation of individual stitches, this work covers the embroidery surface with pieces of colored material, superimposed with a few stitches. No other needlework is more attuned to the fast rhythm of today's world, which demands instant accomplishment. At times, we must forego our speedy ebullience and slow its pace in order to search for more elegant effects achieved by coordinating and over-lapping colors. It is a triumph of color: light shades on sheers for graceful effects, and bright, striking colors on tougher materials, attaining the chromatic audacity of patchworks.

The material and thread

Stitching around the outline in appliqué work is an elementary technique. The only difficulty involved in appliqué work is transferring the appliqué without distorting it and thus altering the design. The design must be reproduced on the basic cloth as well as on the pieces of colored fabric which will be applied to the corresponding shapes. It is wise to remember at the beginning that every appliqué must be cut on the same grain as the basic material in order to facilitate the work and prevent ugly bulges from occurring after the first laundering. Great freedom is given in the choice of colors, bearing in mind that both the background material and appliqué must have the same basic texture. Never apply too heavy a fabric on sheers, although the reverse may be done if you are careful. The best thread is one strand of mouliné in the exact shade of the appliqué it is supposed to outline.

The preparation

Cut the appliqué, leaving a 1/8 inch seam allowance all around (to be folded under), tack in place with a basting, and proceed with the outlining stitch, using the needle to roll the excess fabric

A towel set in which the combination of heavy terrycloth for the basic material and cotton organdy for appliqués is rather courageous. The appliqués are made in successive layers, one petal at a time, from the outer edge to center. The appliqués are sewn to the material with details in satin stitch and short and long filling stitch.

under as you work. If the appliqué is large and has a regular shape, you may fold the edges under in advance and place it on the basic material after it has been ironed and basted. The center of large appliqués should have embroidered details such as lines or dots which fasten the appliqué more securely and prevent a laundry bulge.

If the motif is a mosaic of different colors overlapping one another, you begin the sewing process

Below: a pretty tablecloth on which the strawberry colored, dotted spirals and bows blend delightfully when worked with a very thick and regular Paris stitch. On the right: a detail of it. On the next page: a tablecloth with embroidered appliqués of gardenias in organdy and silk.

with the piece which is underneath all the others, adding the remaining ones in an established order determined by careful observation of the one you are copying. The finished work is then carefully pressed on the wrong side, ironing with the grain of the fabric to avoid wrinkling.

The stitches for appliqué work

Current trends place great emphasis on appliqués which represent a spot of color almost invisibly fastened to the basic material. Consequently, Paris stitch and hemming stitch are used most often; others, such as cording, Turkish stitch and blanket stitch are also suitable for appliqué work in different adaptations.

Paris stitch

Versatile and practical Paris stitch is the unmatched interpreter of appliqué works. Its airiness, combined with a certain firmness, make it the most suitable and widely used stitch. Work from right to left: bring the needle out of the material very close to the fold of the appliqué, then an oblique stitch into the appliqué, and so on.

Hemming stitch

Even though less perfect and more simple than Paris stitch, hemming stitch becomes a necessity on certain materials, such as terrycloth or very firm fabrics, or when the appliqué has irregular edges and requires very distinct contours.

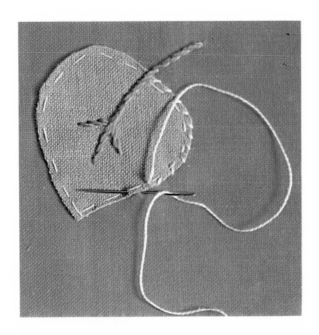

This is also worked from right to left: insert the needle obliquely, take two or three threads of the basic material and two or three of the fold of the appliqué. The deeper the indentations in the contour, the smaller and closer the stitches.

Below: an enlarged version of Paris stitch showing the movement of the needle. Above: the movement of the needle in the more simplified hemming stitch.

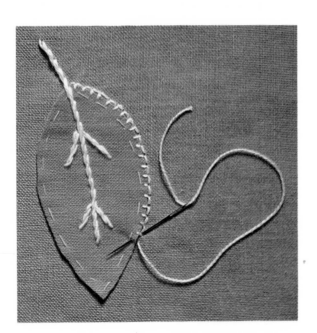

CORDED APPLIQUÉ WORK

Another important interpretation of appliqué work is the one which utilizes a cording. This method is too heavy for a fabric on fabric appliqué, but is perfect for the application of lace, which needs to be supported and guided around the outline. This is necessary to bond the lace to the material with sufficient strength to withstand heavy laundering without distorting the appliqué.

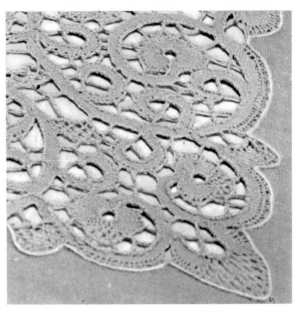

The preparation

Preparation must be very accurate and precise. It is not a waste of time to measure the distance between appliqués, or the appliqué and the edge of your table. In fact, a truly elegant cloth is always custom-sized to the table on which it will be used. In this way, you will receive the full effect of the workmanship and design.

Baste the appliqué first with long stitches; then,

On the next page: a graceful pink linen tablecloth in which the appliqués are emphasized with a cording which prevents distortions and overloading. Above: a detail.

very closely, 1/2 inch from the outer edge, firmly secure the outline of the appliqué in place with a hemming stitch; then use a cording of short, close, but not overlapping stitches which are worked from left to right with the needle entering from top to bottom. After removing all the bastings, trim away any frayed edges with small, sharp, slightly curved scissors.

SOUTACHE BRAID APPLIQUÉ

Here the appliqué work displays its most elementary version; instead of creating the appliqué itself, ready-made soutache braid is applied to a pattern already traced on the fabric. When guided by a sensible design, the effects are outstanding. The timeless styling of soutache braid blends as easily with modern functional furnishing as it does with more formal backgrounds. It is used as accent decoration on cornices, drapes and spreads.

The design

The position of the line which forms the base of the pattern must be established with utmost precision. In the use of a circular design, the fastest and most accurate method is as follows: fold the fabric into four equal parts, creasing the folds with a light pressure of your fingernail to obtain the exact center of the circle; then, holding one end of a tape measure at the center point, place a piece of tailor's chalk at a pre-determined distance (radius) to the outer edge of the circle and slowly rotate tht tape from this fixed point, marking an exact circle with the chalk.

How to apply it

The ribbon or braid is applied by hand with a simple backstitch, choosing the most elaborate part of the braid for entrance and exit points of the needle to hide the stitching. However, the most important operation is the preparation; even if the braid follows a very simple pattern, it must be firmly basted along its entire course before backstitching. Naturally, a more adept craftsman may find pinning the braid to be sufficient.

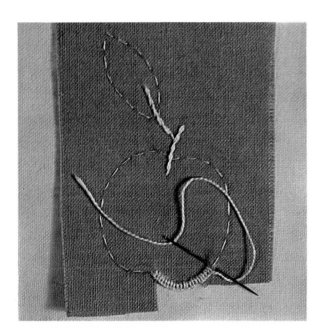

WHEN THE OUTLINE IS THE FOCAL POINT

Occasionally, the contour of the appliqué is not content in the second place role of obscure assistant and demands a more important position requiring embroidery. We then choose either Turkish or Paris stitch, each in its enlarged version. This is, naturally, only applicable to designs which follow regular or geometric courses, carry only a few colors, and have sharp, clear contours.

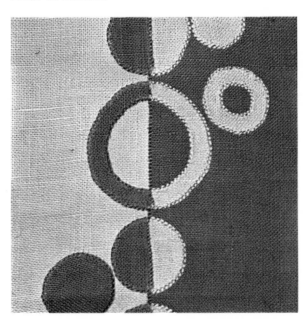

The preparation

The motifs must be cut on the same grain as the fabric area on which they will be applied. Baste them in place first, then use a rapid fastening stitch around the edge. If they are to be embroidered with Paris stitch, fold the material under and fasten with a thin hemming stitch using thin thread. If the motifs are to be embroidered with Turkish stitch, you must trim the appliqué as much as possible and fasten it with a stem stitch.

Paris stitch, in its enlarged version, needs longer

stitches with greater emphasis placed on the horizontal stitch which underlines the edge and must be repeated twice using perle thread. Turkish stitch, explained in detail on page 70, will also increase size and thickness of the thread, leaving its technique unchanged.

On the previous page: a tablecloth with a soutache braid appliqué. Above: the elegance of an abstract design in alternating colors for a table runner. On the lower left: a detail. On the top left: if the appliqué is fixed with a blanket stitch, the excess material can be trimmed away beforehand.

THE BRIGHTNESS OF PATCHWORK

Patchwork was born in America during pioneer times. In those heroic days every piece of cloth was a precious commodity to be used and re-used. Scraps of worn out clothing were pieced together with admirable diligence to form the mosaic-like bedcovers which hold a well deserved place in today's museums as true monuments to patience. It is amazing that these pioneer women could find time to cultivate such outstanding, domestic virtues, since old time western movies generally depict them as busily reloading their husbands' guns during Indian attacks, chopping wood or driving the wagons. Today, patchwork has turned intellectual and dedicates itself to surrealistic geometrics and does not match colors and fabrics casually, but chooses them with a careful, studied casual taste.

On the most modern stark white furnishing, the brilliance of the new style patchwork blends harmoniously; it has abandoned the old, traditional schemes and dedicated itself to a surrealistic approach.

How to make it

In today's fashionable homes patchwork is a colorful addition. In order to carry out the most authentic version, it is first necessary to decide the dimensions of the cushion, draw it on a sheet of paper, and trace the work plan on it. Avoid very small motifs, select instead checks, lines, or geometric figures such as hexagons.

Checks and lines are relatively simple; hexagons need a preparation in which you draw the entire plan of the finished cushion on a base of light cloth. Each hexagon is cut from the various fabrics, leaving 1/2 inch seam allowance, which is folded over a shaped piece of cardboard and pressed on the wrong side. They are then basted in place on the basic material and joined together with a hemming stitch or thin cording. If the patchwork is intended for a child's bedroom, you will have to reinforce the seams with a sewing machine, making a slight quilting between the surface and the lining.

ALL ABOUT SMOCKING

Smocking is an elaborate, but very charming stitch which is not used to decorate table-cloths, bedcovers, or other household items; instead, it covers a world of children's clothing, little girls' dresses and shirts. In English the term "smock" includes a child's shirt, artist's coverall, or short overblouse used around the house.

Recently, smocking and its honeycomb variation have jumped into high style since fashion re-discovered and adopted it for the innocent-sophisticate look.

Preparation

Smocking is based upon painstaking preparation which ensures successful completion of the work. Hasty or careless preparation will result in crooked work which will be impossible to adjust afterwards. Its exceptional character begins with the quantity of fabric to be embroidered; it must be started three times the width desired after smocking. For example: for a front 8 inches wide, you will need 24 inches of material. The excess width is gathered with horizontal running stitches that are pulled to the desired width for smocking; this represents the base on which the actual smocking is developed.

The design

The horizontal rows of running stitches must be made with strictest, geometric ccuracy, as the threads, when pulled, must create exact, vertical lines of gathers. This perfection is not a casual occurrence, but is guided by a precise plan of action. On the wrong side of the fabric, mark many rows of dots across the entire width to be embroidered, taking care that the dots are in vertical as well as horizontal unison. The distance between horizontal dots should be 1/4 to 1/2 inch, depending on the degree of gathering desired, and the distance between rows of dots approximately 5/8 inches. These specifications are naturally to be adjusted in different cases in order to conform to classic or enlarged sizes, or qualities of material.

Whenever possible, the choice of a material printed with regular motifs, checks, or dots simplifies the dotting operation. If, on the contrary, the material is a solid color, it is advantageous to use special carbon paper which is printed with rows of perfectly aligned dots for hot iron transfer and can be purchased in art needlework departments. When using this method, be extremely careful to lay the paper exactly on the fabric grain lines.

You may also use a sheet of graph paper for marking; perforate the paper at regular intervals and carry it along the fabric, pressing a sharply pointed pencil into the holes.

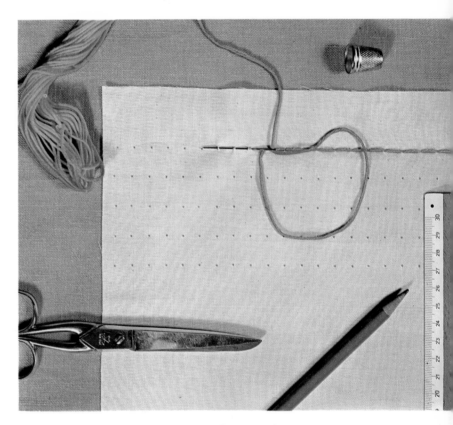

Smocking is worked on a base of horizontal running stitches which must be placed on the fabric very carefully.

Notwithstanding all the other possibilities, an excellent combination is still ruler, pencil, and patience!

Operation running stitches

The next delicate step is to pull the running stitches to form the gathers or pleats. This is done on the right side of the work, and experience has taught us to use the needle as an aid in lining up the pleats as the threads are pulled. After pulling all the running stitches, fasten the first and last ones to the desired length, then adjust and fasten all the others. At the conclusion of this fastening operation, a few short, sharp, vertical pulls on the fabric will arrange the pleats in proper order. After smocking, all the running stitches will be removed.

The thread and material

The choice of fabrics suitable for smocking is not as limited as it would seem; in fact, this stitch adapts to cotton muslin, poplin, silk, silk and wool crepe, woolen muslin, and many others of similar texture. Since the play of the thread on the surface of the pleats or gathers represents the stitch itself, use a rather conspicuous thread. Perle is very good for cotton embroidery and mouline is better for lighter versions and for the honeycomb stitch.

The thread required for the running stitches is also very important and it is advisable to use size 50 sewing thread. It is also mandatory that the lengths of thread be calculated in advance, as the stitches will not gather properly with a knot along the row.

The smocking

After finishing the preparatory phase, you can begin the true smocking on the right side, which is an overall pattern of decorative stitches tied together to give the work a certain elasticity. Smocking has four basic stitches (which allow great leeway for personal interpretations when combined to create dynamic and fancy borders). However, it is advisable to stay within the bounds of rather strict rules.

The keys to smocking

In order to avoid wasted energy in a search for personal compositions, it is best to clarify at the outset the foundation on which the smocking technique is based:

● On stitches that have an upward movement, keep the thread down; in those with a downward movement, keep the thread up.

● On stitches having a horizontal movement, keep the thread down for a left slant; keep the thread up for a right slant.

On all stitches, the needle is inserted into the

● the fabric from right to left.

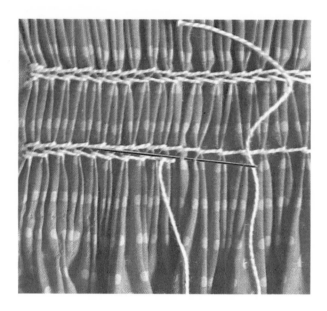

How to work the stem stitch

This is the very basic stitch, elementary, but very useful to complete or frame more complicated motifs. Work from left to right, inserting the needle from right to left under each pleat, keeping the thread tension rather loose for maximum elasticity. You can work with the thread up or down, creating a different effect with the slant of the stitches. A less classical, but more elastic version, is made by taking two pleats at one time.

In the picture above: stem stitch in smocking requires a movement similar to the classical stem stitch, but takes up a pleat with each stitch. On the next page: two little dresses, one enriched by a front almost completely worked with smocking, the other with honeycomb.

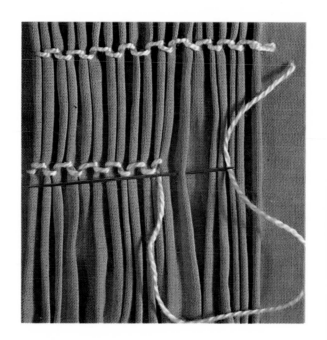

How to work the Van Dyke stitch

This is the most representative of the group, very resourceful and versatile, which creates most of the borders in conjunction with cable stitch. Work from left to right, entering the pleats from right to left. Start with thread down and work across three pleats, one at a time, moving diagonally upward on each of them. Move the thread above and

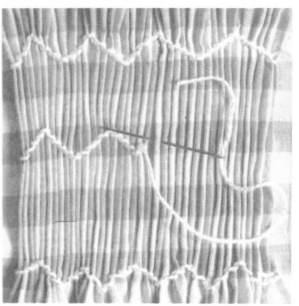

How to work the cable stitch

This is another basic stitch which shows a certain independence as it successfully creates decorative borders by using various colors. Work from left to right, taking each pleat slightly above and below the row of dots alternately, thus forming a series of parallel and very elastic running stitches.

Above: on the left, cable stitch; on the right Van Dyke stitch. Below: on the left, Van Dyke stitch

in two colors on a printed background; on the right, the same stitch worked to form diamonds.

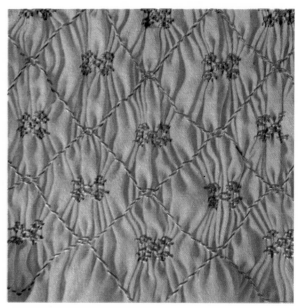

take one horizontal cable stitch on a parallel line to close the motif. Work the same movement over the next three pleats in a downward direction, keeping the thread up. After finishing these three pleats, move the thread down and work a horizontal cable stitch for closing. Naturally, the number of stitches going up and coming down determine the sharpness of the points, while many close and interchanging rows create diamonds.

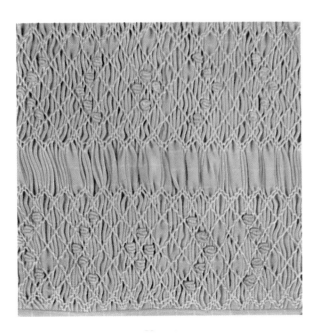

Above: left, a thicker version of Van Dyke stitch with diamonds; right, how to work chevron stitch. Below: left, Van Dyke and chevron stitches combined; right, chevron stitch.

How to work chevron stitch

This is fast and easy to learn if you keep the rules guiding the up and down movement of the needle uppermost in your mind. Work in two rows, each one from left to right.

Row one: Take the first and second pleat together with a right to left horizontal stitch, keeping the thread down, and bring the needle out between the two pleats. With the thread down, take the third pleat on the upper row of running stitches, move the thread up and take a horizontal stitch through the third and fourth pleats. Go upward again, taking the fifth pleat and joining it to the sixth pleat and so on.

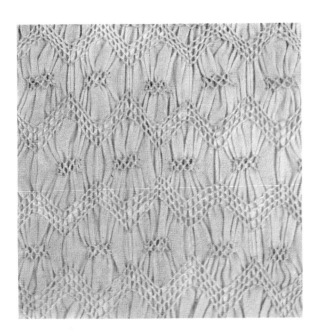

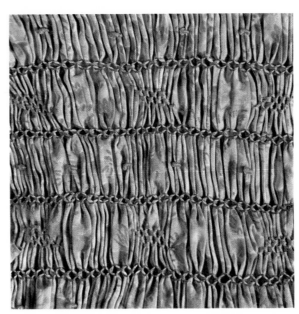

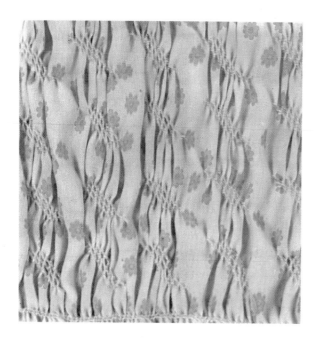

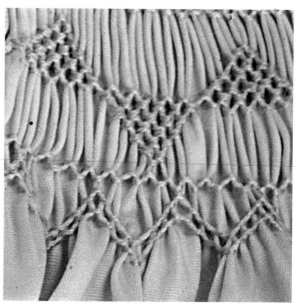

Honeycomb

Honeycomb stitch is an individualistic variation of classic smocking. It takes the same basic preparation, but joins the pleats with very discreet, almost invisible stitches, and the needle passes mainly on the wrong side of the work. The results are so unique that its use has recently been expanded from children's clothing to adult clothes on which it is embroidered with larger stitches.

Above: left, an interesting diagonal application of chevron stitch; right, a circular combination of Van Dyke and chevron stitches. Below, a honeycomb has been used to gather the ruffles of pink dress. (Full view on page 91.)

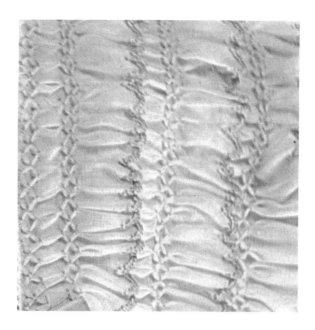

How to work honeycomb stitch

The classic honeycomb consists of a series of ties proceeding from right to left which join the pleats, two at a time, with two horizontal stitches. After joining two pleats, the needle passes on the wrong side, from right to left, and reaches the next two stitches that it joins with the same horizontal stitch. The one drawback to this system, however, is that the finished work loses the elasticity which was its greatest advantage.

It is better, therefore, to use the alternating tie method which proceeds in the opposite direction (left to right) and is the normal technique of all smocking stitches. The needle emerges from the center of the first pleat and with the thread above, joins it to the second one with two horizontal stitches. The needle then re-enters the second pleat and moves along the wrong side of the work to the upper row of running stitches, where it

Work row two the same as row one, reversing the chevrons to form diamonds. The cable stitches which meet in the center must never overlap, but unite side by side to form one stitch.

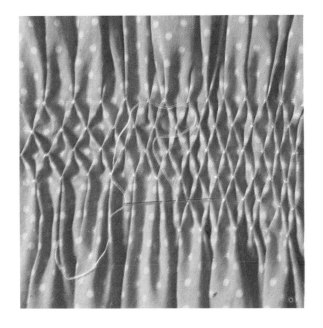

emerges, and with thread down joins the second and third pleats. It then re-enters the third pleat and moves down on the wrong side to emerge on the lower row for joining the third and fourth pleats and continues in this zig-zag manner to the end of the row. Each ensuing row is worked in the same manner, alternating to form the honeycomb diamonds.

Above: the most popular version of honeycomb is the one that proceeds with alternating ties. Below: the honeycomb replaces the pleats. On the following page: a pretty infant's dress in which circular smocking is greatly emphasized.

Circular smocking

At last, we arrive at the most complicated version of smocking: the one embroidered on a circular yoke around those delightful shirts or dresses found in every infant's wardrobe. What new grandmother can resist the temptation to make at least one of them with her own hands? Smocking finds its true justification in the rounded shape, for it was originally designed to gather the width of the material around a neckline.

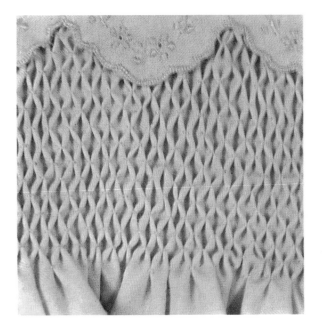

The preparation

For rounded smocking, the preparation is more involved: the quantity of running stitches on the wrong side must be the same in both the shortest row, which is close to the neckline, and in the longest or outer row of the yoke. Consequently, the stitches must fan out and the space between stitches increases proportionately. To avoid complications, it is best to prepare a pattern of the entire area to be dotted on a sheet of tissue paper. Determine the number of rows of running stitch you require, than draw a corresponding number of concentric circles on the paper. Draw the basic row of dots on the smallest circle at the usual distance, and then gradually spread them apart on succeeding circles. If you are unable to judge the distance by sight, use a tape measure to assist. When all the dots are completed, lay the paper on the wrong side of the fabric and mark it by pressing a sharp pencil point through each dot. Always remember that the motifs will be thicker in the upper part and larger in the lower part, since the running stitches are placed farther apart.

BEADED EMBROIDERY
IS GLAMOROUS AND ELEGANT

Sequins, beads, rhinestones, and many other kinds of stones are used to make the most stimulating and fascinating of embroidery works. The splendour of beaded embroidery excites the imagination, and every woman is attracted to anything scintillating and colorful. This embroidery is a loyal ally to high fashion which uses the relief, brightness and color of the stones for an additional effect on its most prestigious models. Its execution is not difficult; nevertheless it requires a very well controlled taste, a continuous, inventive talent that will prevent it from becoming too theatrical or ornate. For this reason, there are designers who expertly use the large selection of stones at their disposal, choosing them for their shape, color and size, constantly inspired with contemporary, refreshing ideas.

The design
Beading is very often done without a design and is created free hand by the embroideress' imagination. In the event that a design is to be used, it is transferred by perforated pattern to the right side of the work if stones of different qualities are to be hand sewn on the fabric. If, on the contrary, the beads are uniform as in the case of sequins, you can attach them to the fabric with a hook and the design is therefore reproduced on the wrong side of the fabric.

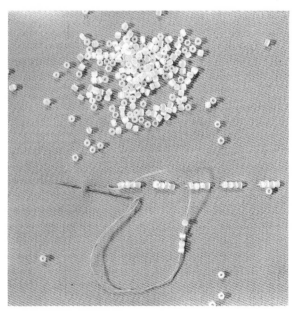

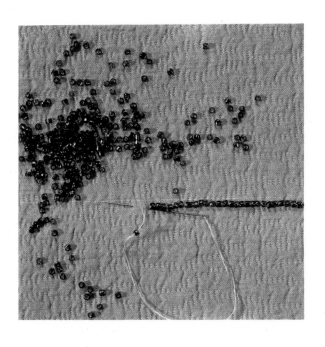

Two different ways to attach beads to the fabric: on the orange material, one at a time with a back stitch; on the green material, in groups with a running stitch.

The material and thread
Since embroidering with stones is almost exclusively limited to cocktail or evening dresses, the most suitable fabrics to receive it are traditionally chiffon, silk, lace, faille, velvet, and for special summer evenings, shantung, linen, or jersey.
Bead embroidery also attains excellent results on opaque and firm materials for shoes and evening

handbags. For beaded embroidery the eye of the needle must be as fine as the thread in order to pass through the small holes in the various stones used. Nylon thread is widely used and is available in a vast selection of colors. It is very difficult to avoid broken threads, or loosening of knots when the dress is worn, which can result in a true disaster. It is therefore advisable (fabric permitting) to lightly brush the material with a mixture of fabric glue and water, on the wrong side, while still attached to the frame.

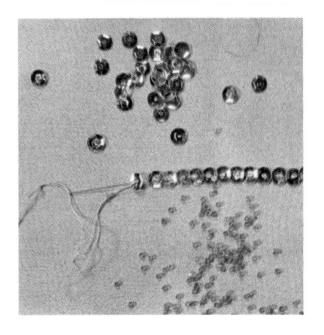

In the picture below: a very lavish border of stones, beads, and pearls. In this particular rendition, the tear drops and crystal drops fall free. Above: hand-sewn sequins, applied one at a time.

Use the frame

It is important to remember that any embroidery with stones must be done on a rectangular frame, as this is most suitable for holding the wide surfaces of blouses, shirts or dresses.

The stones

There are many different types of stones available for embroidering and the manufacturers constantly produce new ones in conjunction with the fashion creators. They are divided into three main groups: *pearls*, which come round, oval smooth, boroque, pear-shaped or drops, can be transparent or opaque, and come in many sizes, from the tiny seed pearl to the tubular bugle; *sequins*, small discs of brilliantly colored plastic, either flat or cup-shaped, which are fastened to the fabric through tiny holes in their centers; *stones*, gleaming irridescent and colored crystals, cut like pre-

cious stones, easily sewn to the material through holes in the stones or metallic settings. All this splendor is directly attributed to a man named George Frederick Strass, who had an idea to imitate diamonds synthetically around the middle of

the 18th century.

There are also many fantasy shapes like leaves, stars, crescents and tiny bells, all containing a pinpoint hole for easy fastening to the fabric.

How to work on the right side to attach stones

Small stones are attached, one at a time, with a backstitch: pull the needle out of the fabric; then place a bead on the needle, make a backstitch;

In the picture below: another elegant creation, entirely in shades of topaz on a pearl grey silk background, in which traditional and non-traditional stones counter-balance effectively.

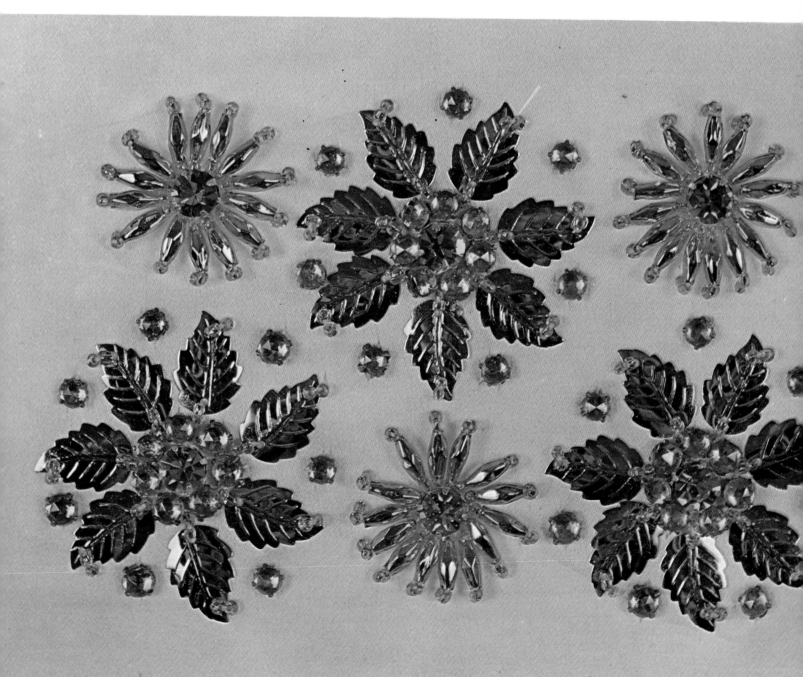

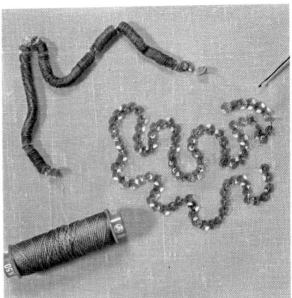

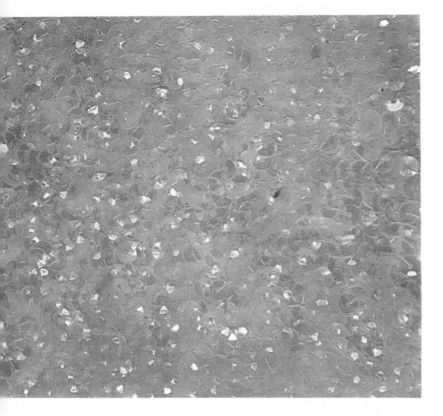

The two sides of the appliqué when working with a hook: in the picture above right, the right side of the work; here, below, the wrong side.

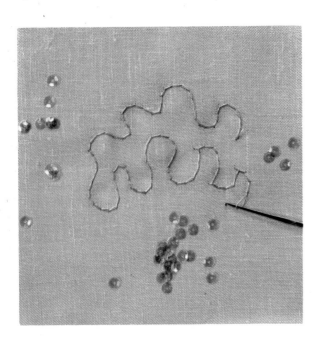

then another bead on the needle, another back-stitch, and so on. They may also be attached in groups with a simple running stitch: pull the needle out of the fabric, thread four beads on the needle, and re-enter the fabric making a running stitch on the wrong side, corresponding to the length of the beads, and start again to thread the beads.

Sequins are attached one at a time with a back stitch when you desire a close, overlapping look. If you wish them spaced separately, pull the needle out of the fabric, through the hole in the sequin, place a small bead on the needle and pass the needle through the sequin hole. An interesting detail to note: to accelerate the work, professional seamstresses do not insert the needle into the beads one by one, they plunge the needle into a boxful of beads and spear one or two halfway up the needle.

How to work on the wrong side to attach stones

When stones of uniform size are used for borders or textured work, they are attached to the right side of the material from the wrong side of the work. Transfer a whole string of sequins to a spool of thread and, holding them in your left hand under the frame, push them along the thread to the fabric, one at a time, while your right hand pushes a very thin metal crochet hook through the fabric, catches a loop of the thread between the sequins, and draws it back out. This will form a series of loops on the wrong side.

TRUE NEEDLEPOINT

Needlepoint is an activity which has exceeded the popularity of embroidery as it is understood in its traditional sense and has taken an important place as an engrossing hobby and relaxing therapy! As a matter of fact, it is no longer considered a strictly feminine occupation; many British and Scandinavian men are dedicated to this pastime.

There are some people who fondly recall the sight of Somerset Maugham embroidering needlepoint in the grand hall of the Gritti Hotel on the Grand Canal of Venice, one of the most exclusive haunts of the international set. Architect Henry Van De Velde, industrial designer and leading craftsman in the field of interior design, created original designs for needlepoint as well as embroidering them himself.

Working needlepoint is very similar to painting; the application and concentration provide the same deep, intimate pleasure. It is a relaxing and hypnotic exercise as the colored threads slowly trace and compose a design.

Although it is considered very fashionable today, it was born a few centuries ago in France under the name of Gobelin. In Italy it achieved its greatest splendour by royal craftsmen, embroidered on yards of tapestries the size of entire walls, with designs of woods and countrysides on elegant backgrounds. Other famous artisans used to design cartoons in needlepoint. The 19th century brought a trend toward flower themes which still maintain a place of high esteem today.

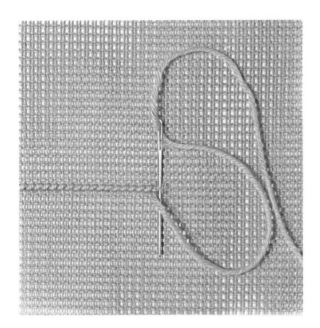

The thread

Needlepoint is embroidered with yarn; in drab, antique colors for the classic Gobelin version, in brighter tapestry yarns for more modern applications, or with mouliné for more elegant effects. For the more ambitious artisans who wish to reach the ultimate elegance, tapestry yarn and mouliné thread are interspersed with dramatic results. It is important to work with short threads to avoid gnarling which results in twisted stitches. Use a blunt tapestry needle.

On the opposite page: an eyeglass case made on single thread canvas with mouliné thread. This page: on the left, the movement of needlepoint worked left to right. Below: worked from right to left.

Importance of the canvas

The quality and size of embroidered tapestries are directly attributable to the canvas used for the work. Needlepoint generally prefers the double-thread canvas for practical designs with modern taste, which blend harmoniously with today's settings. Single thread canvas may be used for those fine miniatures called petit point, although considered to be rather old-fashioned today. Single thread canvas takes endless patience, and often causes eyestrain; the resultant lack of a proper setting for such energies makes it hardly worth the effort. The double thread canvas, accordingly, although a bit on the rough side, is advisable, and gives great satisfaction and enjoyment.

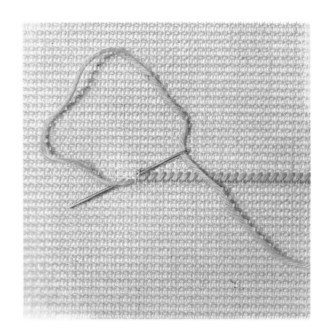

The frame is essential

Canvas works and the frame are co-existent. A frame prevents a crooked work which is difficult to straighten, or irregular thread tension and uneven surface. It is also useful for the finishing stage of fastening threads and brushing with fabric glue as suggested for embroidering with stones. The work must not be ironed, but the right side should be treated against spots with the special spray which also waterproofs.

The design

Needlepoint designs cannot be reproduced by traditional methods because of the particular characteristics of the canvas. It requires the design to be drawn on a piece of graph paper in which each square corresponds to a hole in the canvas and is copied point by point.

There are stamped designs in colors - like the 1850 original on page 101 - and designs in black and white. In this case, you will have to use representa-

tive symbols to distinguish the colors. For instance, a cross indicates color red, a dot for blue, a circle for green, etc. In order to copy the design with a minimum of effort, establish the center of both the canvas and the drawing; then, divide each surface into fourths or eighths by drawing pencil lines on the drawing, and basting threads on the canvas. Embroider the design only, in each section, leaving the background for last. When the entire design is completed, check your work against the drawing, row by row (with the help of a magnifying glass if necessary), and then fill in the background.

Stamped canvas

Just in case the prospect of such detailed concentration completely destroys your vision of relaxing therapy, don't panic. Needlework shops and departments have the answer to each individual requirement. Canvases are available with pre-stamped, colored designs on them. You simply match the thread color to the colored holes on the canvas, and you're on your way with no eyestrain, no headaches. This type of canvas also allows for a degree of personal interpretation in the shading of colors, which results in a feeling of self-sufficiency and a personalized creation. These canvases

are available in many sizes at moderate prices; also in kits which contain all the necessary yarn and are the favorite of most beginners. There are even more elegant canvases imported from France containing designs and color suggestions which are both fashionable and authentic.

Needlepoint is adaptable to many different subjects by varying the thickness and size of the canvas and, consequently, the thread. On the previous page: a canvas in which the floral motif can be interpreted many different ways. Above: even jewels can be embroidered on petit point. On the left: a detail.

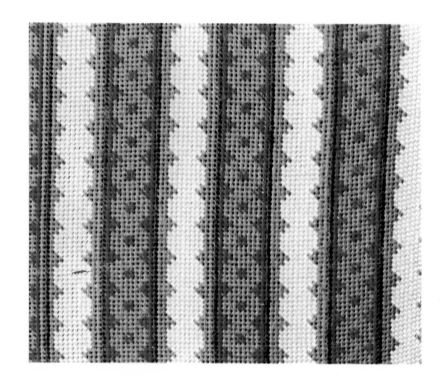

Selecting a needlepoint design

The choice of needlepoint designs available range from very small items, generally destined for obsolescence, to larger canvases for handbags, slippers, telephone book covers, hassocks and pictures. An originally designed piece is, of course, the most elegant, for it will eventually become a cherished heirloom.

Without a doubt, one of the most successful achievements is still the canvas chosen to cover the seat of a favorite chair in the average home. For the classic 19th century style, choose a rather rich floral motif that stands out on a solid color background; or, a wreath with a textured motif that conforms to the shape of the chair if it is 18th century. When applying the canvas to the chair, remember to use the shiny brass upholstery nails for 19th century styles, and the duller, more baroque nails for the others. The background color is of prime importance, as it must emphasize and not overpower the central motif. In addition to the classic off-white background, current fashion favors the bright purples, deep blues and forest greens.

A common pitfall to avoid is the temptation to overdo and waste your energy embroidering four or six chairs, or even an entire living room. One small chair next to a buffet table or in a foyer will provide a dramatic, yet casual effect.

How to work needlepoint

Needlepoint is very easy as it is one rhythmic, repetitious movement, guided by the canvas. Begin the work at the lower left, inserting the needle from top to bottom under each thread of canvas until it is entirely covered with thick, close, fabric-like stitches. For photographic reasons the needle movement has been summarized into one phase; actually, the right hand inserts the needle and the left hand, under the canvas, regulates the thread tension and passes the needle back out, one thread below, while the right hand pulls the needle out.

Small motifs can also be embroidered in two-way rows: when reaching the right hand side, reverse the direction of the needle and insert it from upper right to lower left. However, in order to ensure more even and regular stitching, it is best to turn the work upside down and continue to work from left to right.

The one-way direction is mandatory for embroidering the background.

Note: when starting and ending new threads, work them through the back of the work with a running stitch.

The background and the motifs

The central, colored motifs must be embroidered first, then the background and spaces between motifs. Prepare various needles, each one with a different color thread and proceed, using them alternately and skipping from one area to the next on the wrong side of the work, thus avoiding the frequent cutting of threads. Another, wiser method, is to work all the shades of one color in an area, then change to shades of the next color in the same area. The easiest system to use is one color at a time, skipping across the back of the work to different areas.

When needlepoint abandons its characteristic floral motifs, it does not suffer any loss of elegance. On the preceding page: a geometric, textured type of workmanship. On this page: an elegant daytime handbag.

AN EXCELLENT HOBBY: THE TAPESTRY STITCH

Tapestry stitch is quick and easy, and after a very short period of practice, a new talent is mastered with a minimum of effort. It grows rapidly enough to grant even a novice to needlework the joy of starting a project and finishing it within a few hours. For this reason, tapestry stitches are referred to as "tranquilizers."

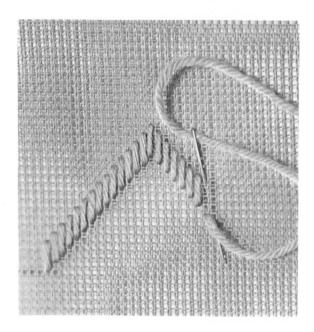

The design

There are no patterns for tapestry stitches. They are generally borrowed from finished works, cleverly copied, or originally designed by the professionals The only method is to use a piece of graph paper (as in needlepoint) and mark the length and direction of the stitches.

How to work tapestry stitch

The family of tapestry stitches develops freely by matching long, short, long and short, vertical or diagonal stitches that create an endless selection of constantly changing motifs in limitless color combinations.

What to embroider

The field for tapestry stitch application is even wider than the one for needlepoint. Tapestry stitch has abandoned the miniature class and is freely used in its various versions throughout the field of house furnishings on a multitude of items like waste baskets, book covers, cornices and placemats, as well as for chair seats, pillows and decorative wall hangings. All this is enriched and personalized by the imagination and ingenuity of the craftsman.

Above left: tapestry stitch acts vertically on a given number of holes, establishing a pattern as it moves. Below: a detail of the address book shown on the left of the next page.

The canvas and thread

Single thread canvas is used for tapestry stitches. It is available in different sizes, determined by the requirements of the finished work but is always rather firm. Tapestry yarn, woolen yarns and sometimes mouline are the most suitable threads. Since the success and prestige of all canvas stitches depend on the proper matching of colors, remember that the colors appear darker after working than when in the skein.

ment does not appeal to you, there is no reason why you cannot make both movements with your right hand. Simply insert the needle with your right hand and reach underneath to return it again. Your left hand still remains underneath the work to gauge the thread tension as the stitches are concluded. It becomes an almost mechanical rhythm after a little practice.

Above: the cover of this address book required a modern design; nothing is more suitable than the hexagon motif in shades of bright colors. On the right: a subtle idea for a curtain tie-back, made with a tapestry stitch, using four shades of the same color to create an interesting contrast to the transparency of the material.

Tapestry stitch is always worked on a frame, from left to right, without knots on the wrong side. Start and end new threads by passing a running stitch through the finished work. Push the needle out of the canvas with your left hand while your right hand passes it back again a few holes higher or diagonally, depending on the chosen pattern. If you are a beginner and the ambidextrous move-

How to work the flame stitch

Flame stitch is the only one possessing a true pattern, steeped in tradition, a direct descendant of motifs on the antique covers of high, straight back, renaissance chairs. The best plan is to begin with the entire first row of color; succeeding rows follow the pattern of the first, each one changing only

The classic flame stitch also adapts to unusual applications. In the left picture: a pair of indoor scuffs. Below: a detail. Above: a handsome, oval-shaped magazine holder for the den or family room.

color. Since the main characteristic of flame stitch is the waves of color, it is best to avoid contrasting colors and work several shades of one or two colors. When using several shades of two colors, separating them with a row of white will brighten the work and also, when interpreted in a modern key, the antique flame stitch takes on a polished appearance, making it adaptable to today's decor, without losing its traditional quality.

CLASSIC AND PRECISE: THE CROSS STITCH

Cross stitch is the unacknowledged patriarch of all canvas stitches. It is the precise and colorful main character of many fashionable embroideries, from the most naive to the ultra sophisticated, always rich in charm like the painting stitches.

The thread

If you are cross stitching on canvas and must cover the web completely, use smooth, woolen yarns or tapestry yarn; it must, above all, be in proportion to the material used on any application. The crosses must be well visible, neither overlapped nor too sparse.

The design and material

The traditional cross stitch requires a material with prominent threads as it proceeds by counting threads. Penelope canvas is the classic material when thin materials or thick materials too dense to count are abandoned. Make a carbon paper transfer to place tiny crosses on the fabric. Naturally, you must follow the vertical and horizontal grain of the fabric as accurately as possible when transferring the crosses. If the fabric is an especially elegant one which you are afraid to spot with carbon paper, just baste a strip of thin gauze over the area to be embroidered (on the straight grain) and use this as a guide for counting threads.

How to work cross stitch

The classic execution proceeds horizontally in two movements. First, work from left to right, making a series of stitches slanting to the right, inserting the needle from top to bottom; then, return along this row with the same movement in the opposite direction, crossing the right slant stitches with a left slant. While this system is more rapid and thread tension remains more even, it has one disadvantage: since you do not get a complete picture of one area, it is impossible to correct a mistake

Even when embroidered in multi-color, cross stitch attains a certain elegance, especially when based on an interesting design. Here you see, for example, a beautiful linen tablecloth, enhanced by a group of fruit in clear, shaded colors.

In the picture below: the cross stitch is made in two movements; one from left to right starts the half cross and the second from right to left completes it. Above: a detail of the tablecloth on the preceding page revealing its dual role, elegant or casual, depending on the setting.

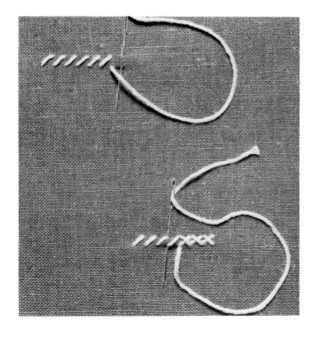

in the pattern while making the stitch. The old fashioned method crosses one stitch at a time as follows: working from left to right, bring the needle out on the lower left of the first cross, pass the needle down four threads above and four threads to the right; bring the needle out again four threads to the left, pass the needle back down four threads below and to the right; this slant stitch crosses the first slant stitch.

THE ART OF CROCHET

Crochet is a much more delightful pastime than embroidery. It is so soothing and relaxing that even the unaware spectator falls prey to its hypnotic spell. The ultimate purpose of the finished object is secondary to an avid crochet fan; the primary purpose is to amuse oneself and keep idle hands busy with this pleasant, geometric game.

A more demanding and practical technician, who loves to finish things in a hurry, can crochet exquisite items of clothing and unique creations in the home furnishings field. Publishers constantly print new needlework magazines which contain photographs of finished works complete with detailed directions which minimize the interpretive effort.

Nevertheless, the designers of those beautiful items seem to assume that every crocheter possesses sufficient knowledge and skill to interpret the abbreviations, idiomatic phrases, and numerous asterisks. In order to enable you to learn these symbols and to enjoy the beauty of the more difficult works, this chapter will give you a simple gradual entrance to the hospitable world of crochet, expressed with many descriptive pictures.

SELECTING THE YARN

Printed crochet instruction books always specify the exact quantity and type of yarn needed to make each garment. The most precise ones indicate the trade-mark or brand names as well, since the designation of three-ply, four-ply, etc., does not establish the weight of the yarn precisely. The term "ply" merely indicates the number of strands twisted together in that particular yarn and not the weight or volume.

Generally speaking, there are two main types of yarns: the casual type, which consists of fingering yarn, sport yarn, worsted, baby yarn, etc.; and specialty yarns, which include the mohairs, bouclés, tweeds, bulkies, etc. Manufacturers are constantly adding new varieties to each of these groups. However, crochet prefers the smooth twisted yarns which emphasize the stitches. The fancier, textured yarns tend to overpower the crochet work.

In the picture opposite: a group of specialty yarns showing lamé, angora, mohairs, and chenille. Above: a group of colorful sport yarns.

The casual group

This group of yarns is generally the mainstay of crochet work. Within this general classification you will find smooth, all wool yarn in many different weights, orlons and nylons also in a variety of weights, and the cable-twist yarns which can be had in solid colors, tweeds, or textures.

The specialty group

These yarns are more elegant and expensive, although not all of them adapt to crochet work well. They are all unusual yarns, dramatic, strikingly effective, and used mostly for dressy clothes. This group includes the lames, angora, chenille, organdy and silk ribbon, and many different types of mohair.

A GOOD START FOR EXCELLENT RESULTS

The success of crocheting depends a great deal upon the enthusiasm and personality of the person who attempts it. You must always comply with a preliminary series of set requirements which include the choice of the type of yarn and proper hook and at least an adequate mastery of crochet language.

Selecting the proper hook

There are no set rules for this, as each crocheter works differently from the next. In order to compensate for this, you must make a gauge on the exact yarn, stitch, and hook which you plan to use on your garment, and adjust the size of the hook to meet the specifications of the instructions. In a generalized manner, we can then say that steel crochet hooks range in size from 00 to 12; the higher the number the thinner the hook. A hook numbered 00 is generally used on 4-ply worsted, and a size 6 or 7 on fingering yarn. You will learn to be your own judge.

Crochet abbreviations

Printed instructions always use abbreviations for common terms occurring throughout the directions, and you must familiarize yourself with these. The basic key is as follows: st, stitch; ch, chain; * to *, repeat the directions written between the two asterisks. The last symbol is the most important one, used most often, and must be clearly understood or you will become bogged down in a hopeless sea of confusion. Other symbols will be explained throughout this chapter.

How the work progresses

Crocheting proceeds very simply from right to left, then turned at the end of the row and the same process repeated. There are a few exceptions to this basic method when working items that are round or tubular. The Tunisian or afghan hook is also considered a crochet hook, but uses a different method. This is worked on two-way rows; loops are picked up and retained on the hook across one entire row, then worked off two at a time on the second row and the work is never turned.

Position of the hands

A crochet hook is held like a pen, between the thumb and index finger of the right hand, guided by the middle finger. The left hand holds and controls the thread, looped over the index and small finger, in position easily accessible to the hook. After a little practice, the hands will assume the proper position automatically.

How to start

Crochet is started with a long chain the required length for the garment you are making. An initial loop is knotted with your hands before inserting the hook. Place the hook inside this loop and pass it under the thread which is on the index finger of your left hand and draw it back out, forming a new loop on the hook. This is the first chain and you will continue this same procedure until you have made a chain the desired length. This basic starting chain always has a tendency to tighten up and it is therefore advisable to use a size larger hook on this row.

Stitch gauge

Stitch gauge is of primary importance; at the same time, it is a variable thing due to the differences in the hands of each crocheter. In order to properly establish a precise gauge, you must first make a sample of the stitch you wish to use with the proper hook and the yarn you plan to use in the garment. To do this, chain (ch) 30 and work several rows of the pattern stitch. Measure the sample from side to side and divide the number of stitches on the

row into the exact measurement of the row; this will determine the stitch gauge or number of stitches (sts) you crochet per inch. If you are following printed directions and your gauge is inaccurate, change the size of the hook until you maintain the same gauge. If you are improvising on your own, simply multiply the number of stitches per inch by the desired number of inches. For each new project, a gauge must be established.

In the picture below: how to work the basic chain stitch. It is a good rule to use a larger hook for the first row than the one required for the rest of the work.

In the pictures to the left and above: the position of the hands for crocheting. Obviously, after mastering the movements of the hook, the position of the hands during the phases of the stitch will become spontaneous and natural.

BASIC CROCHET STITCH

The basic stitches are a single crochet (sc) and double crochet (dc) with several variations. The pattern of these two stitches is used to create an unlimited variety of stitches either by combining the two or in the manner by which they are worked into previous rows. In order to begin to familiarize you with the abbreviations, we shall now begin to use them in conjunction with the explanations. "Yarn over hook" (YO hook) means to take up the thread, which is on your left index finger, with the hook. "Draw up a loop" means to draw the hook and the thread back through the previous stitch or loop. "Draw through loops on hook" means exactly what it says and completes the stitch.

Slip stitch (sl st)
Insert the hook into basic chain (ch), yarn over hook (yo hook) and draw through both loops.

Single crochet (sc)
Place hook in chain, yarn over hook (yo hook) and draw up a loop in chain, yarn over hook again and draw through both loops.

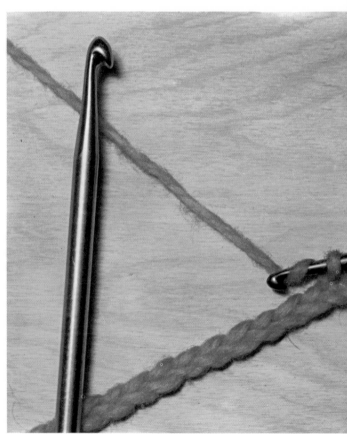

In the picture above: movement of the hook in slip stitch. On the right: single crochet (sc) differs from slip stitch by one more movement.

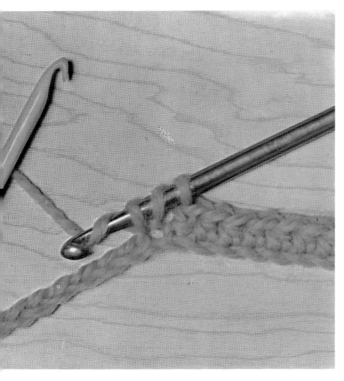

In the picture above: half double crochet (hdc); on the right: double crochet (dc). The difference between these two stitches is also one movement. movement.

Half double crochet (hdc)

Yarn over hook, insert hook into chain, yarn over hook and draw up a loop, yarn over hook and draw through all 3 loops. The half double crochet (hdc) and the slip stitch (sl st) are both generally used to complement other stitches.

Double crochet (dc)

Yarn over hook, insert hook in chain and draw up a loop, yarn over hook and pull through 2 loops, yarn over again and pull through last 2 loops.

(Picture 1) Starting Row: Make a loose chain desired len[gth] and sc into second ch from hook, *skip 2 ch, work 5 dc i[n] next ch, skip 2 ch, sc into next ch*; repeat bet *'s across r[ow] ending with 3 dc into last ch, ch 1 and turn. Pattern R[ow:] Sc into first dc of row below, *work 5 dc into sc of row bel[ow,] sc into 3rd dc of 5 dc shell below*; repeat bet *'s, end[ing] with 3 dc into last sc of row below. Repeat pattern row on[ly.]

(Picture 2) Starting Row: Make a loose ch desired length and work 7 dc (shell) into 3rd ch from hook, *skip 3 ch, work 7 dc into next ch*; repeat bet *'s across row ending with 4 dc into last ch, ch 2 and turn. Pattern Row: *Work 7 dc into space between the 2 shells of row below*; repeat bet *'s across row ending with 4 dc into turning ch, ch 2 and turn.

(Picture 3) Starting Row: Make a loose chain desired leng[th] and work a sc into ea ch, ch 1 and turn. Pattern Row: Wo[rk] a sc into ea st of row below, ch 1 and turn. Repeat patte[rn] row only.

(Picture 5) Starting Row: Make a loose ch desired leng[th] and work (4 dc, ch 3 and sl st) into 3rd ch from hook, *sk[ip] 4 ch, work (4dc, ch 3, sl st) into next ch*; repeat bet *'s en[d]

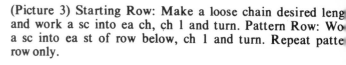

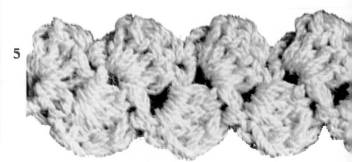

OTHER EASY STITCHES

(Picture 4) Starting Row: Make a loose ch desired length and work 1 dc into 3rd ch from hook, *skip 3 ch, work (3 dc, ch 1, 1 dc) into next ch*; repeat bet *'s, ending with ch 3 and turn. Pattern Row: Work (3 dc, ch 1, 1 dc) into ch 1 sp of shell below*; repeat bet *'s across row ending with 1 dc into turning ch of row below, ch 3 and turn. Repeat Pattern Row only.

(Picture 6) Starting Row: Make a loose ch desired length and work 1 sc into 2nd ch from hook, *dc into next ch, sc into next ch*; repeat bet *'s, ending with dc in last ch, ch 1, turn. Pattern Row: *Work 1 sc into dc of row below, 1 dc into sc of row below*; repeat bet *'s, ending with dc into last st, ch 1, turn. Repeat Pattern Row only.

(Picture 7) This stitch is worked in alternating rows of single, then double crochet. Row 1; Work a sc into ea st ending with ch 2, turn. Row 2: Work a dc into ea st ending with ch 1, turn. Repeat rows 1 and 2 for pattern.

ing with ch 3, turn. Pattern Row: *Work (4 dc, ch 3, sl st) into ch 3 sp of row below*; repeat bet *'s across row ending with ch 3, turn. Repeat Pattern Row only.

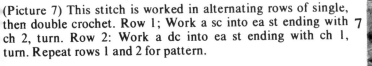

OTHER IMPORTANT DEFINITIONS

Every slight or subtle variation of the basic stitch is extremely important in crocheting. For example, an isolated chain stitch can represent the base for an elaborate lace stitch; while inserting the hook in a different manner can create a modification leading to an entirely new stitch.

Entering the stitch below

Unless otherwise indicated, the hook is inserted into the center of the stitch in the preceding row directly under the 2 top threads. There are also other ways to enter the stitch that create variations which follow.

The rib stitch on the left and the Rumanian stitch below are variations of the classic single crochet. Each is worked by inserting the hook in the back loop of the stitch below.

The chain loop

The chain loop is used in forming open or lacy patterns. It is exactly what the name implies: an open, chained loop between two stitches.

The turning chain

At the end of a row, directions always stipulate "ch 1 and turn", "ch 2 and turn", etc. Since the thread is always at the top of a crochet stitch, when turning the work to start the next row, it is necessary to make a chain long enough to reach to the top of the next row. Without this turning chain, the sides of the work would either pull too tightly or be irregular. Thus, we use a ch 1 for turning if the next row is to be single crochet or a ch 2 for double crochet.

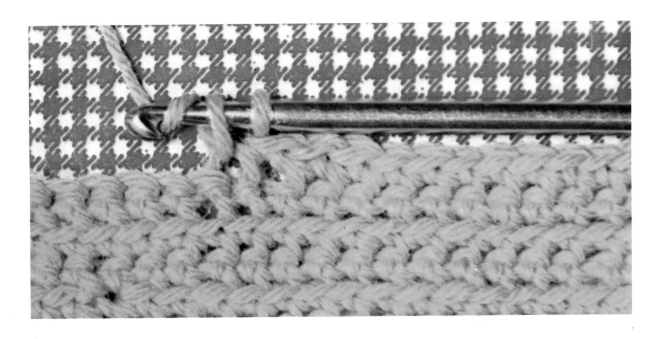

The Albanian stitch (above) and the Russian stitch (on the right) are also single crochet stitches. They differ from the others because the hook is inserted under the front loop of the stitch below.

• *Rib stitch:* Work each row in single crochet, inserting the hook under the back loop only. Ch 1 and turn at the end of each row.

• *Rumanian stitch:* Work the same as the rib stitch but do not turn at the end of the row. Break the thread at the end of the row and start each row from the right side.

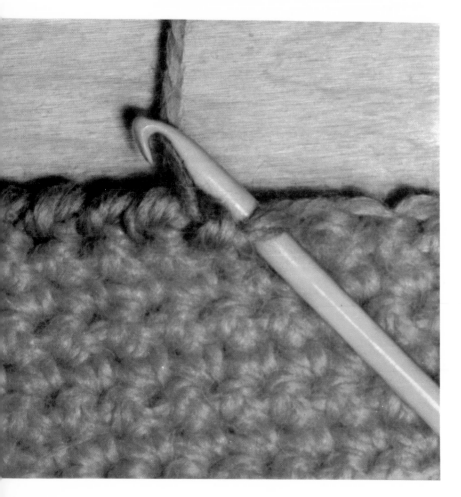

● *Albanian stitch:* Work each row in single crochet, inserting the hook under the front loop only. Chain 1 and turn at the end of each row.

● *Russian stitch:* This is the regular single crochet; break the yarn at the end of each row and do not turn.

● *Raised double crochet:* This is a regular double crochet, but the hook is passed behind the 2 vertical bars of the stitch below instead of into the top of the stitch. (See photo above.)

● *Shrimp stitch:* This stitch is used only for a finishing touch on edges. It is a regular single crochet worked in reverse; i.e., from left to right, inserting the hook in the top of the edge stitch.

The raised double crochet (above) is one of a group of textured stitches. The hook is inserted in back of the stitch below. On the left: shrimp stitch, very popular for a finishing detail.

A FABRIC MADE OF CROCHETED RINGS

One of the most pleasant aspects of crocheting is that you can utilize its technique to create many things normally considered outside the field of true crochet work. Covered rings is one ingenious invention, widely used to make gay place mats, coasters, heat-proof table mats, and even some outstandingly creative room dividers. Common curtain rings are covered with single crochet, using thick, colored thread or yarn. At the end of the round, slip stitch into the first stitch and leave an end of thread for sewing. When all of the rings are covered, thread a wool needle with these ends and invisibly sew the rings together on the back of the work. Many variations are possible by combining rings of different sizes. The place mat shown here is made of uniform rings assembled in alternating colors of strawberry and white.

INCREASES AND DECREASES

If you have decided to devote your time to crocheting a garment such as a sweater, blouse or dress, you will now have to learn to shape the square which you have already mastered. This is very easily accomplished by increasing and decreasing either on the side seams or within the body of the work itself.

Increasing at the side edges

In order to increase 1 stitch at the beginning and end of a row, simply work 2 stitches into the first and last stitch. On the following row, work them in the regular manner and you will have increased 2 stitches on this row. If more than one stitch is to be added at the side edge, simply ch 1 more than the desired number of stitches to be increased and work a stitch in each chain before continuing across the row. For example: to add 2 stitches to the next row, ch 3, turn and work 1 stitch into each of the 2 chains between the hook and the last stitch of the previous row.

In the picture on the left: increasing 1 stitch at the side edge. Below: increasing 2 stitches on the side edge which creates a zig-zag. Unless this broken edge is necessary for a particular design, always distribute the extra increases within the body of the row.

Increasing at a corner

In order to increase at a corner, tie a thread marker to the corner stitch; work across the row to the marked stitch and place 3 stitches into this corner stitch. On the next row, work across in the regular manner. If you wish to increase on every row, use the 2nd of the 3 stitches as your new corner stitch on the next row.

On the green sample: increasing within the row. On the blue sample: increasing at the corner.

Increasing within the row

Tie a colored thread marker at the point or points where you wish to place the increases and work 2 stitches into 1 when you reach the marker.

Decorative increase within the row

After placing your markers, work up to the marker and make a ch 1 between the 2 stitches. On the next row, work a stitch into the chain.

A decorative increase on the corner

Work across the row to the marked point and place a ch 2 between the two stitches. On the next row, work 3 stitches over this chain.

CHENILLE REQUIRES A SIMPLE STITCH

Lush, velvety chenille is one of the few fancy yarns suitable for crocheting, and produces rapid results. Only simple stitches are suitable for working chenille, as in the case of this handbag made entirely of a single crochet and edges finished with a shrimp stitch.

For the small two-toned purse illustrated, two or three skeins of each color chenille should be sufficient. An old worn envelope type purse makes an ideal ready-made frame. Measure the length from the lower edge of the flap, up over and down the back, up to the inner edge of the front. Crochet a long rectangle with bands of contrasting color, then work 1 row of shrimp stitch completely around the edge on the right side. Pin in place over the frame, and with invisible stitches, fasten the new cover to the old purse.

Decreasing at side edges

To decrease at the beginning of a row, simply skip the first stitch; at the end of the row, skip the next to the last stitch, work the last stitch, make a turning chain, and proceed normally across the next row. In order to decrease 2 stitches at once on a side edge, work to within 2 stitches of the end of the row, skip the next to last stitch, slip stitch into the last stitch, make a turning chain; on the next row, skip the chain and work the next regular stitch, then proceed across the row.

Decreases at a side edge should have a smoothly angled contour even if this edge is to be sewn to another (picture below).

Decreasing within the row

Work across the row to the place marked for decreasing and work two stitches together as follows: draw up a loop in the next stitch, draw up another loop in the following stitch, yarn over hook and draw through all three loops. To decrease a double crochet, yarn over hook, draw up a loop in next stitch, draw up another loop in the following stitch, yarn over hook, draw through 2 loops, yarn over hook, draw through 3 loops on hook. An easier method is simply to skip the stitch to be decreased.

In the picture above: a right angle decrease. In the picture below: decreasing within the row.

Decreasing a corner

To make a right angle decrease, simply skip 2 stitches on every other row at the marker. For a sharper angle, skip the 2 stitches on every row.

PLACE MATS IN PEZZOTTO WORK

Pezzotti rugs, indigenous to the Italian Alps, are characterized by colorful variegated strips. A very successful imitation of this regional work is done with crochet. These rustic place mats in fall colors are a good example of the work. They are used in a casual setting with pottery dishes.

The entire mat is worked in single crochet; the color bands are worked in groups of four two-tone rows. On each row within the first four-row band, move one color 2 stitches to the right as illustrated; on successive four-row bands, divide the two-tone bands at different places. When finished, this will give the mat its characteristic variegated appearance. When all the bands are completed, work 1 row of single crochet completely around all four sides.

TECHNICAL DETAILS

If you are crocheting a garment, there will be technical details concerning necklines, buttonholes and shaping. The finesse with which these are accomplished determines the degree of perfection you will achieve.

How to work V neckline

To work a V neckline, you must mark the center of your work first and then decrease each side separately. Shaping is done on the right side of the work; skip the next to last stitch at the end of the row (left side of neck) and skip the first stitch at the beginning (right side of neck) of the row. For a wider V, you may decrease every row, and for a sharper, elongated V, decrease every fourth row.

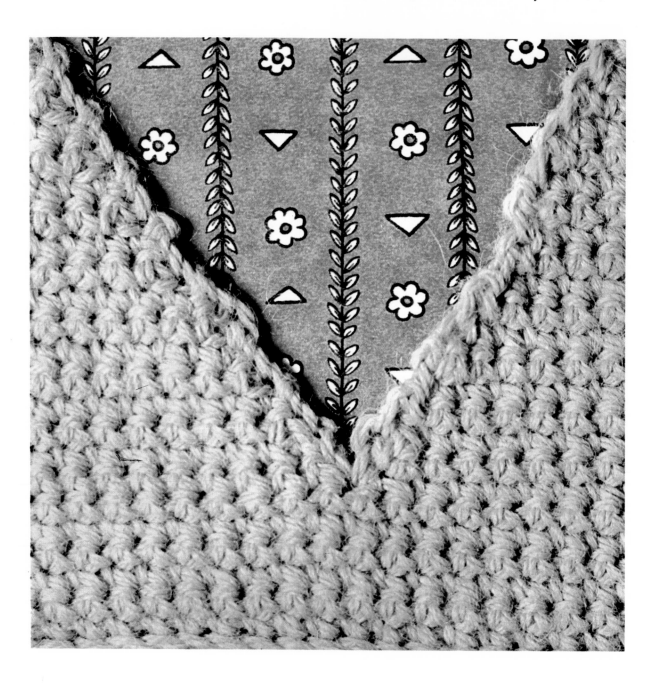

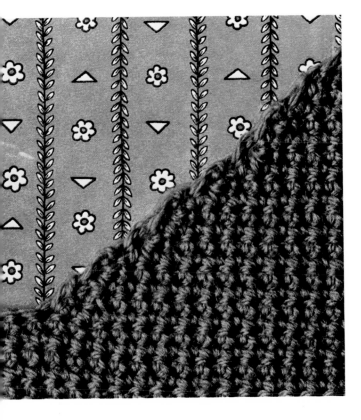

next row. On the following row, begin to decrease 1 stitch at the beginning and end of every other row until the cap measures 1/2 the armhole measurement when a ruler is placed at the underarm row. Bind off 2 or 3 stitches at the beginning and end of each of the next 2 rows, leaving approximately 3 to 4 inches across the last row.

In the picture below, the horizontal buttonhole. This simple method does not have to be re-worked with a buttonhole stitch and is explained on the next page.

The irregular appearance of the edges on a V neckline are unavoidable, even by expert workmanship; however, this will be perfectly smoothed over when the finishing row of single crochet is applied.

The cap of a sleeve (pictured above) regulates the line of the entire sleeve. The shaping must therefore be neither too sharp nor too rounded.

How to shape the sleeve cap

The sleeve cap is that part of the sleeve which is above the underarm and must be worked to very definite measurements. Bind off 1 inch of the work at beginning and end of the same row by slip-stitching across the inch at the beginning of the row and working to within 1 inch of the end of the row; make your turning chain and proceed across the

How to work horizontal buttonholes

On the right side of the work, skip as many stitches as necessary for the button to pass through, and chain a corresponding number to replace them for the next row.

How to work vertical buttonholes

Measure the number of rows necessary for the length of the buttonhole by placing the button over the work, and mark the stitch which must be left open. Work across the rows on one side of the stitch first, then the other, and on the next row work straight across to close the buttonhole.

The vertical buttonhole (picture below) is worked by separating the stitches and crocheting several rows, one side at a time, before reconnecting the row.

How to work pockets

Make the pocket opening about 4-5 inches wide in the same manner as the horizontal buttonhole. When finishing the garment, work a pocket band across the front of the opening for about 1 inch and sew a ready-made pocket lining inside.

How to work buttons

To cover a button, chain 3 and join with a slip stitch; work 6 single crochet into chain and connect with a sl st. On subsequent rows, increase in every other stitch until the required diameter for a specific button. Work 2 rows even, place the button inside and then decrease on each row, instead of increasing, to close the back. This button shape may also be stuffed with a padding instead of a button.

Covered buttons provide an indispensably elegant touch to crocheted garments. The buttons pictured here were all crocheted over button forms.

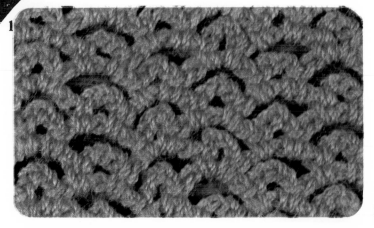

(Picture 3) This pattern is a multiple of 12 sts. The p directions are for one pattern plus 5 end sts. We suggest you practice on a sample chain of 20 starting first st in 3 from hook. When ready for a larger piece of work, s start and end each row with 3 dc instead of 5, using the in the repeat. Starting Row: * Work a dc in ea of next

(Picture 1) Starting Row: Make a chain desired length and sc into second ch from hook, * ch 4, skip 3 ch and sc into 4th ch, ch 3 and sl st into sc (1 shell and picot))*; repeat bet *'s across row, ending with ch 5, and turn. Pattern Row: sc into top of first shell, ch 3 and sl st in sc for picot, * ch 4, sc in top of next shell, ch 3 and sl st in sc*; repeat bet *'s across row ending sc in top of last shell, ch 5 and turn. Repeat pattern row only.

(Picture 2) Starting Row: 1 dc in 3rd ch from hook, * ch 2, 1 dc in ea of next 3 ch *; repeat bet *'s, ending with dc in ea of. last 2 ch, ch 2 and turn. Row 1: * 5 dc under ch 2 of row below *; repeat bet *'s, ending with dc into top of turning ch of row below, ch 4 and turn. Row 2: * 1 dc into ea of center 3 dc of shell below, ch 2 *; repeat bet *'s, ending with ch 1, dc in top of turning ch of row below, ch 2, turn. Row 3: 3 dc into ch 1 of row below, * dc 5 under ch 2 of row below *; repeat bet *'s, ending with 3 dc under turning ch of row below, ch 2, turn. Row 4: 1 dc under ea of first 2 dc of row below, * ch 2, 1 dc in ea of center 3 dc of shell below, repeat bet *'s ending with 1 dc under ea of last 2 dc, ch 2 and turn. Repeat rows 1-4 for pattern.

ch 4, skip 3 ch, sc in next ch, ch 4, skip 3 ch *; work a ea of next 5 ch, ch 2 and turn. Row 1: * 5 dc, ch 2, sc in 4 loop below, ch 4, sc into ch 4 loop below, ch 2 *; repea *'s, ending with 5 dc, ch 2 and turn. Row 2: * 5 dc, 6 dc into ch 4 loop, ch 1 *; repeat bet *'s, ending with ch 2 and turn. Row 3: * 5 dc, ch 4, sc bet 3rd and 4th dc be ch 4 *; repeat bet *'s, ending with 5 dc, ch 2 and turn. Re rows 1-3 for pattern.

LACY STITCHES

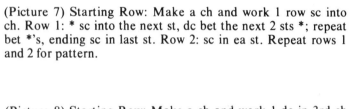

(Picture 4) Starting Row: Make a chain and sc into ea chain. Row 1: ch 2 (retaining all loops on hook), draw up a loop in 2nd ch from hook, in first, second and third st of row below, YO, draw through all loops, ch 2 (eye of st); * draw up a loop in eye of st, in last st just worked and in ea of next 3 sts (6 loops on hook), YO and draw through all loops, ch 2 *; repeat

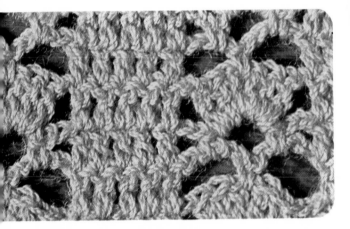

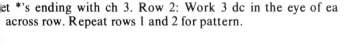

et *'s ending with ch 3. Row 2: Work 3 dc in the eye of ea across row. Repeat rows 1 and 2 for pattern.

Picture 5) Make a chain and work 1 row dc into ch, ch 2, rn. Pattern Row: Work a dc in front loop of ea st across row, 2 and turn. Repeat this row for pattern.

(Picture 6) Starting Row: Make a ch and work sc into ea ch, ch 2 and turn. Row 1: * Work a dc into ea of next 2 sts, ch 2, skip 2 sts *; repeat across row, ending with 2 dc, ch 1, turn. Row 2: * sc into ea of next 2 sts, ch 2 *; repeat across row, ending with 2 sc, ch 2, turn.

(Picture 7) Starting Row: Make a ch and work 1 row sc into ch. Row 1: * sc into the next st, dc bet the next 2 sts *; repeat bet *'s, ending sc in last st. Row 2: sc in ea st. Repeat rows 1 and 2 for pattern.

(Picture 8) Starting Row: Make a ch and work 1 dc in 3rd ch from hook, * ch 1, skip 1 ch, 1 dc in next ch *; repeat across row. Row 1: ch 3, * 1 dc under ch 1 of row below, ch 1 *; repeat across row, ending dc under turning ch. Repeat this row for pattern.

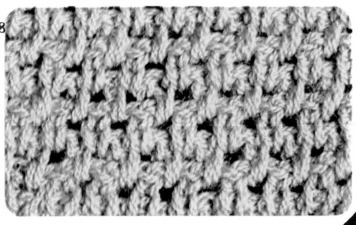

SPECIAL CROCHETED EFFECTS

There are different techniques which utilize supplementary accessories to achieve special effects such as hairpin lace, jacquard weaves, beading and looped fringe. These are the special details used by professionals to enhance their work, so let's learn all about them.

How to work in the round

Many items are started with a circle; keeping it flat and circular is sometimes very difficult unless you are following precise directions. There is a basic method to follow if you are on your own. Ch 3 and close the circle with a sl st, ch 1 (if the next round is to be sc), or sl st, ch 2 (if the next round is to be dc). Work 6 sts into the first round; 12 sts into the second round; space the increases farther

The flat circle (above) has increases interspersed on each round. This method is used for berets, coasters, etc.

apart in the next rounds. You will have to judge exactly how many increases are necessary on succeeding rounds in order for the work to lie flat. Never place increases in the same place as preceding rounds unless you desire a hexagonal or octagonal shape.

How to do tubular work

This is very simple. Make a chain the same length as the diameter of the circle, close with a slipstitch and just continue around the chain in successive rows. The Russian stitch and Rumanian stitch are perfect for this type of work.

The two movements of beading with a crochet hook. Below: the wrong side of the work. To the right: the right side of the work with beads attached.

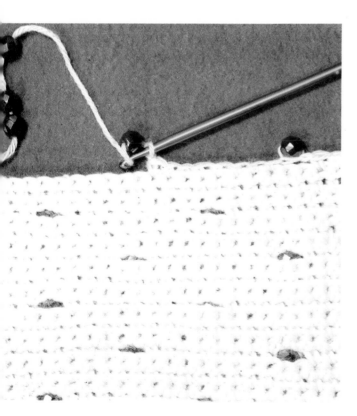

How to work beading

This is a relatively simple technique. First, you must thread the beads or sequins on to the skein of yarn you plan to work with. When using sc, work across the sts to place where bead is required, ch 1, push a bead up to hook, ch 1 again, skip 2 sts and continue sc to next place for bead. The 2 ch sts replace the skipped stitches on the following row; this is done to allow room for the bead to be recessed into the work. When using double crochet, it is not necessary to skip sts; simply push the bead up before the last yarn over to close the stitch.

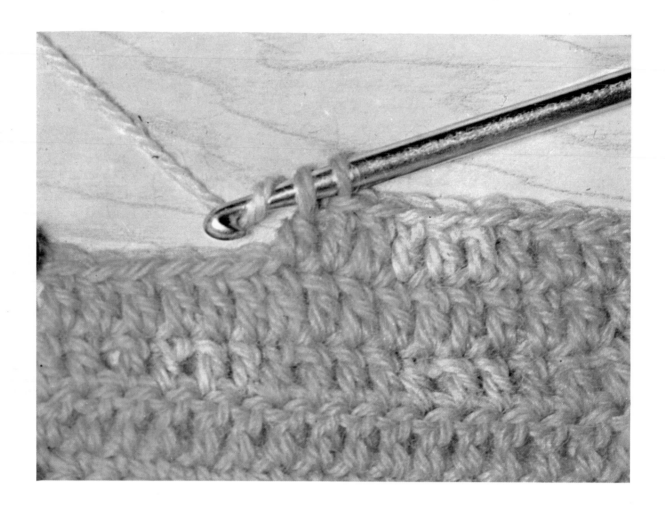

How to work jacquard patterns

"Jacquard" is a simple and concise way to say "changing colors while working." It is possible to create multi-color fabric effects or worked-in designs while crocheting. There is a very easy way to use more than one color without breaking and knotting threads. While working with one color, the color or colors not in use are held in back of the work along the upper edge of the previous row, and the hook picks up the thread in use from underneath the other color; when the stitch is closed, the last loop through the stitch closes over the carried yarn. The last stitch of each color zone

must be closed with the new color about to be worked.

How to work elongated stitches

This is very useful in creating fancy effects and must not be confused with hairpin lace. Start with a basic chain and one row of single crochet. The elongated stitches are always formed on the second single crochet row in this manner: work a single crochet and *draw up a loop of the desired length, remove the hook from loop, insert hook in next st, draw up a loop and sl st *; repeat bet *'s, and end with a series of chain sts long enough to reach to the top of the elongated loops. Turn and work a sc through the top of each long loop.

On the opposite page: how to change colors in Jacquard work. This page: above; lengthening the loops; below; single crocheting through the top of each loop.

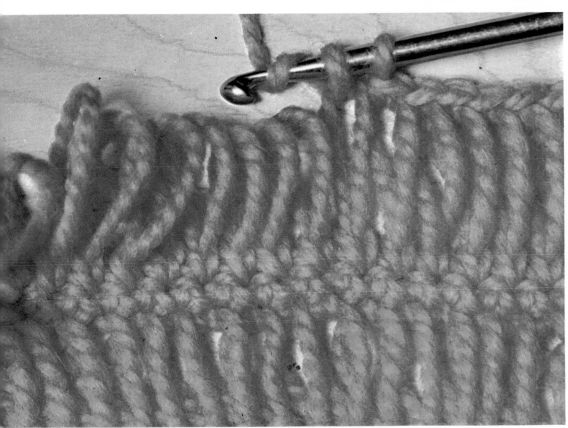

AN ELEGANT CROCHETED EVENING BAG

*This antique look is never out of tune with the fashion picture. Having learned to increase and decrease, you should now be able to duplicate the synthetic silver lamé evening bag below. The simple two row pattern is as follows: make a chain of the desired length for width of purse and work a sc into each ch. Row 1: (star stitch) ch 2, draw up a loop in 2nd ch from hook, draw up a loop in ea of next 2 sts, YO and draw through all loops, ch 1 (eye of star); *draw up a loop in eye of star, in last st already worked, in ea of next 2 sts (5 loops on hook) YO and draw through all loops, ch 1*; repeat between *'s across row. Row 2: sc in ea st and ea eye. Repeat these two rows for pattern. You can purchase ready made frames and linings in art needlework departments and should shape the crochet work to fit over the lining.*

CROCHETING LOOP FRINGE

This is an original and decorative stitch used for many different types of cuffs, borders, and hats. It can also successfully imitate fun fur by using yarns in fur shades.

How to work loop fringe

Use a wooden ruler or strong strip of heavy cardboard to gauge the length of your fringe and work as follows: make a chain of the desired length and work a row of sc or dc into chain for selvege. Insert hook in first st, pass thread over ruler or cardboard (see picture) from front to back; with hook, draw thread from back through to front of st, YO and close st. Continue to work a loop in every stitch along the row, removing the ruler at end of row. If you wish a straight fringe instead of loops, cut through the loops with a sharp scissors before removing the ruler.

For successive rows, always single or double crochet a row between looped row. For a short furry fringe, use a pencil instead of a ruler for your guide.

Crocheting loop fringe. Above: using a heavy cardboard guide for loops. Below: a modern application of the short furry look on the cuff of a basic black dress.

A CASUAL PLACE MAT SET

*These early American style place mats were made with white crochet cotton using 2 rows of colored crochet cotton for the centers. Each square is worked separately and then sewn together with an overcast stitch on the back of the work. With colored thread ch 6 and join with sl st, ch 2. Row 1: * work 4 dc, ch 1 into circle *; repeat bet *'s 3 more times, join. Row 2: work * 4 dc, ch 1, 4 dc, ch 1* under ea ch 1 of previous row, join and fasten off color. Row 3: attach white cotton and work *4 dc, ch 1 under ch 1 of previous row, 4 dc, ch 1, 4 ac, ch 1 into corner ch *; repeat between *'s around row and join. Continue to work in this manner placing 2 dc groups and 2 ch sts in ea corner, 1 dc group and ch 1 under chain sts along sides of square until reaching desired dimensions. After assembling all the squares, work a finish row of sc completely around mat.*

HAIRPIN LACE

The art of making hairpin lace is absorbing and relaxing. It is most famous for elegant, lacy shawls; however, today's fashion designers have gone far beyond its original limitations and utilized hairpin lace for lavish ribbon dresses, angora sweaters, mixed with other crochet stitches, etc. Instead of a crochet hook, you will need a hairpin loom which is sold in several different sizes in all art needlework departments. The size of the loom determines the width of the lace strips which are connected to each other with a simple chain stitch. Hairpin lace strips are sometimes joined together with gold or silver thread for more elegant designs; they may also be scalloped when joining by crocheting several loops together in one stitch.

A soft, dainty stole made of hairpin lace.

How to use the loom

Directions that follow are given European method to conform with pictures. If American method is desired, work loom from open end towards the top. Make a loose chain stitch with a crochet hook, remove hook and place loop on right hand bar of loom (picture on right). Bring thread behind left hand bar and rotate loom over to left (picture below). Insert crochet hook up through loop on left prong, draw thread through and make a chain (left picture page 147). *Remove hook from loop, rotate loom from right to left and fasten new loop

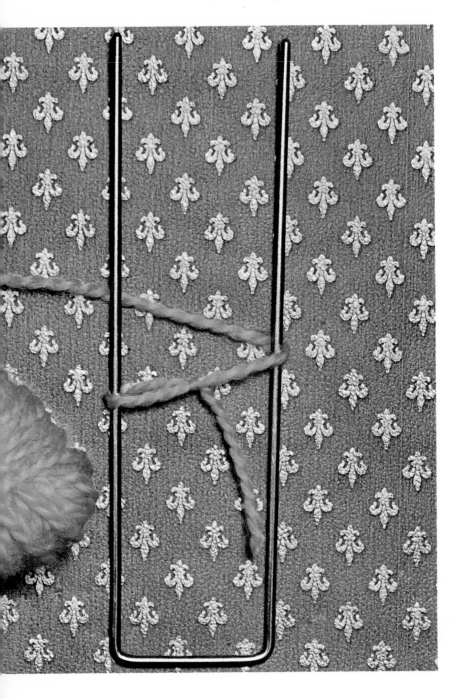

First two phases of working on the loom. Above: right hand prong is inserted into loop. On the left, rotating the loom for first stitch.

with a sc st * instead of a chain. Repeat bet *'s until the loom becomes crowded. When American method is used you can slide finished loops off, leaving last few on loom and continue with work.

Another fastening method

If you wish to have a heavier texture in the center of the hairpin strip the single crochet stitch is fastened over both threads of the loop instead of through the loop. (See blue picture.)

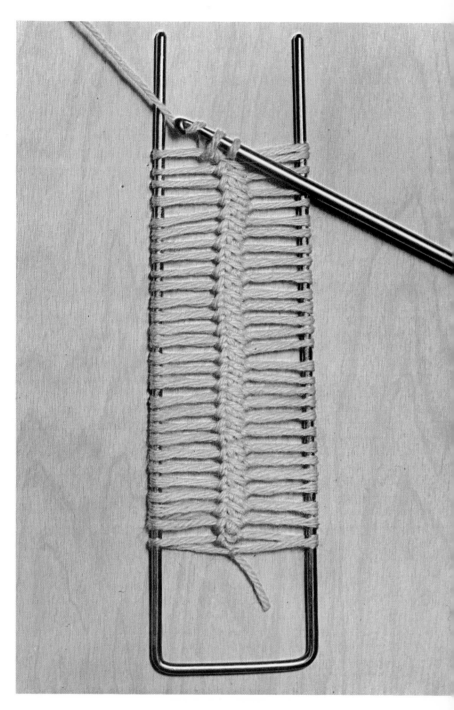

On the left, the hook makes the first fastening stitch. On the right, single crochet over both threads of loop; this can be folded along center and used for irregular fringe.

CHARMING MATS FOR HOT DISHES

These very simple mats have a design created by increasing at regular intervals, directly over previous increases. Ch 5 and join with sl st, ch 2. Row 1: Work 10 dc into circle, join with sl st, ch 2. Row 2: Work 2 dc into each st, join, ch 2. Row 3: Work 2 dc bet first 2 sts, * skip 2 sts and work 4 dc in space bet skipped sts and next one *; repeat bet *'s ending with 2 dc in same sp as first 2 dc, join, ch 2. Row 4: Work 3 dc in center of 4 dc group below, * work 6 dc in center of next 4 dc group *; repeat bet *'s ending with 3 dc in same sp as first 3 dc group, join ch 2. Continue in this manner, adding 2 dc to ea group on every row until mat is desired size. Work 1 row shrimp stitch around outer edges. Make an Irish rose (p. 151) and sew in center.

THE FILET STITCH

In the early 19th century, crocheted filet stitch abounded on curtains, bedspreads, borders on sheets, towels, tablecloths, etc. After decades of obsolescence, it has again returned to fashion on woolen scarves, vests, dresses, and many other items requiring a lace look. The original version was tightly worked with white crochet cotton; today, it has been adapted to all weights and textures of woolen yarn. It is a very simple combination of double crochet stitches alternated with chains.

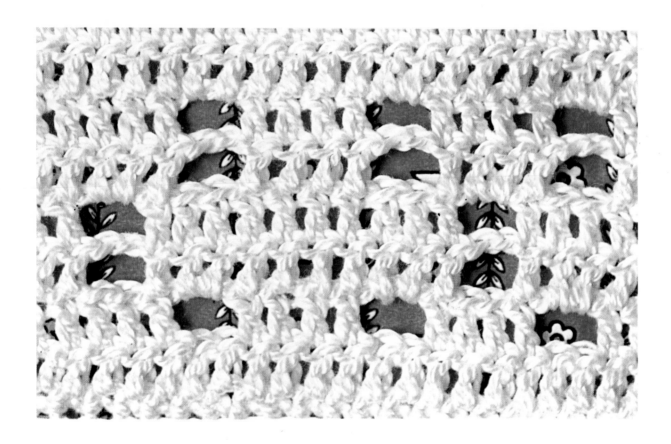

How to work filet stitches

The checkerboard design is the easiest way to start. To begin, chain 20 and work a dc in 5th ch from hook, dc in next ch, *ch 2, skip 2 ch and work a dc in ea of next 2 ch *; repeat bet. *'s ending with dc in last 2 ch, ch 4 and turn. Pattern row: Work 2 dc under next ch loop, ch 2 *; repeat bet *'s ending with 2 dc under ch loop, ch 4 and turn. Repeat the pattern row.

This sample shows the spacing of filets; ch over the skipped sts and replace them on the next row.

Once you have practiced the technique of skipping sts by working a ch over top and replacing the sts on the next row, it will be very easy to make your own pattern designs.

IRISH LACE CROCHET

The original version of this crochet, which began in Ireland, was always a composition of leaves and flowers on a lacy mesh background. The modern, more realistic version features mainly the Irish rose or star on a mesh background. Fashionable interpretations are used in many different yarns; nevertheless, the very thin wool yarns or crochet cotton are most suitable.

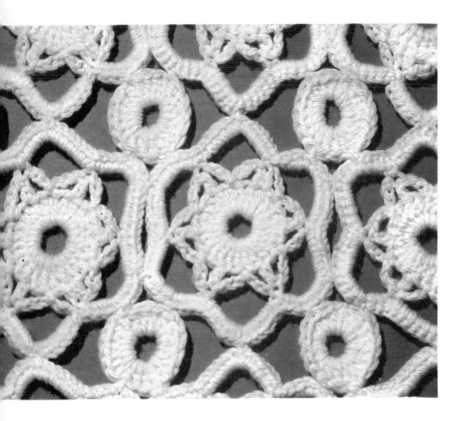

On the right: an elegant table runner in a 19th century setting. Above: a detail of the star.

How to work Irish star
Ch 12, close with a sl st and work 24 dc into ch. Next row: ch 5, skip 1, sl st in next st, *ch 3, skip 1, dc in next st, ch 3, skip 1 and sl st into next st*; repeat bet *'s closing last point of star with ch 3, sl st in 2nd ch of first ch 5. Next row: *ch 10, sl st in top of next dc*; repeat around all 6 points of

star, then work 10 sc over each ch. Fasten off, leaving an end for sewing. The stars are joined on the wrong side with small overcast stitches. The small circles sewn between the stars are made as follows: ch 10, join with a sl st; ch 2 and work 10 dc into ch.

Above: the charming and effective Irish rose enhances other creations. If desired, a third row of petals may be added.

How to work Irish rose

Roses are worked separately, then sewn on to other works for added emphasis. Why not try them on the border of a dress or to decorate and dress up a pretty sweater?

Row 1: ch 5 and join with a sl st. Row 2: work 10 sc into circle, join. Row 3: *ch 4, skip 1 st, sc in next st*; repeat bet *'s 4 more times, join. Row 4: work a sc, 5 dc, sc, into ea ch 4 loop, join. Row 5: (second row of petals) *work a sc in back, inserting hook across the bar bet ch loops of first petal row, ch 5*; repeat bet *'s 4 more times, join. Row 6; work 1 sc, 9 dc, 1 sc in each ch 5 loop, join and fasten off.

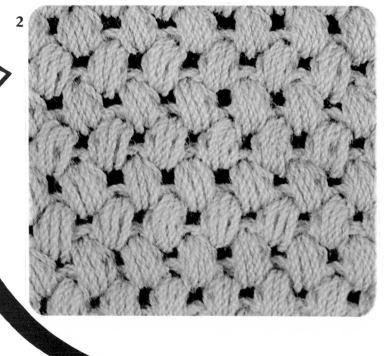

(Picture 1) Starting Row: Make a ch desired length and work a dc into ea ch, ch 2 and turn. Pattern Row: *Work a raised dc in front of next 4 sts by inserting hook horzontally under bar, work a raised dc in back of next 4 sts*; repeat bet *'s across row. (Picture of raised dc on p. 124) Repeat this pattern row 2 more times. On the next row, simply reverse the raised dc (i.e., 4 front dc over 4 back dc and vice versa) and repeat 2 more times. Reverse the rows after every 3 rows.

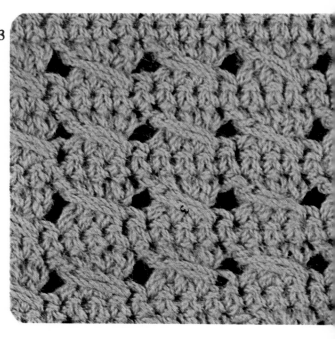

(Picture 2) This is a reversible stitch. Starting Row: Mak ch desired length. In 3rd ch from hook, *YO and draw u loop 4 times, YO and draw through all loops on hook (bubb ch 1, skip 1 ch*; repeat bet *'s across row ending with c turn. Pattern Row: *Work a bubble in the ch st of prev r ch 1*; repeat bet *'s ending with bubble under under turn ch of prev row, ch 3 and turn. Repeat pattern row.

(Picture 3) This is also a reversible stitch. Starting Row: Ma a ch desired length. Row 1: Sc in ea st, ch 2 and turn. R 2: *Skip 1 st, dc in next 3 sts, insert hook back in skippe and draw up a loop lengthening diagonally across the 3 YO and finish sc*; repeat across row, ch 1 and turn. Rep rows 1 and 2 for pattern.

ENWORK STITCHES

(Picture 6) The bubble stitch on row 3 is explained in picture 2. Make a ch which is a multiple of 8. Row 1: Work 1 dc, ch 1, in every other st. Row 2: Ch 3, *work a dc in ea of next 7 sts (counting ch 1 below as st), ch 1, skip 1*; repeat across row ending with 7 dc. Row 3: Ch 2, *2 dc, ch 1, skip 1, bubble in next st, ch 1, skip 1, 2 dc, ch 1, skip *; repeat bet *'s ending with dc in last st. Row 4: Same as row 2. Repeat these 4 rows for pattern.

ture 4) Rows 1, 2, 3: Single crochet in ea st. Row 4: Ch 3, p 2 sts, 2 dc in next st, ch 1*; repeat bet *'s across row ng 2 dc in last st. Rows 5, 6, 7: Single crochet in ea st. 8: Ch 3, *2 dc in next st, ch 1, skip 2 sts*; repeat bet nding with dc in last st.

ture 5) Rows 1 and 2: Single crochet in ea st. Row 3: Ch ip 2 sts, *dc in next st, ch 2, dc in same st, skip 3 sts*; at bet *'s ending skip 2 sts, dc in last st, ch 1, turn. Row in dc below, *sc bet the 2 dc sts, 3 sc in ch loop*; repeat ss row ending with sc under turning ch.

AN ATTRACTIVE ALL PURPOSE AFGHAN

This handsome afghan crocheted in fall colors is a more refined version of the typical plaid lap robe. You will need approximately two hanks each of 6 or 7 colors and an aluminum crochet hook size G. The stitch is all half double crochet (p. 119) and the color pattern is worked exactly like the pezzotto place mats on page 131, changing colors every 13 rows. Start the first row with a ch 100 and work 25 stitches in one color, 75 stitches in another. When choosing colors, select several shades of one basic color and other colors to complement the main color.

TWO-TONE CROCHET

There are bi-color stitches, not included in jacquard work, which require a separate explanation. The most popular and interesting ones are the plaid and check stitches which are really much easier than one may think at first glance.

How to work plaids

Plaids are worked in bands of horizontal color using either a double or single crochet stitch. First, determine the width or widths of these bands and then mark the position of the vertical stripes which are worked in as follows: crochet across to the marker, skip 1 st, ch 1 and continue in this manner to each marker. The vertical lines are embroidered in with either a chain stitch or a double thread back or running stitch.

Working plaids is easy and versatile, (picture below). The checked pattern (above) utilizes two colors in a very original way.

How to work checks

Checked crochet work takes a little perseverance at first, but it soon becomes a fun stitch. Starting rows: with mc make a ch desired length and work a dc in 9th, 10th, 11th ch from hook, * ch 3, skip 3, 3 dc in next ch loop*; repeat bet *'s across row, drop loop and turn. Attach cc in back at bottom of first dc, ch 5, *dc in each of 3 skipped spaces on starting ch, ch 3*; repeat across row ending with 3 dc in bottom of turning ch, drop loop, do not turn. Pattern Row 1: pick up mc loop, ch 5, *work 3 dc inserting hook under mc ch and through dc of row below, ch 3*; repeat across row, drop loop and turn. Pattern Row 2: fold last row down, pick up cc loop of prev row and ch 5, *3 dc under cc loop, ch 3*; repeat across row, drop loop, do not turn. Repeat rows 1 and 2.

SMYRNA STITCH OR HOOKED RUGS

This is the ancient technique for weaving Oriental rugs, modernized and adjusted to fit into the realm of Western patience. Nevertheless, the result is just as prestigious, whether you choose a classic Persian design or one of the art-nouveau designs more suited to today's furnishings.

The rug canvas

The base of the rug is a very heavy double thread canvas with holes 1/4 inch square. Many interesting versions are available in varying lengths and widths in all needlework departments.

If you wish to design your own rug, buy plain un-stamped canvas in desired size and prepare your drawing with the same method used for needlepoint. Each square on a sheet of graph paper corresponds to a hole in the canvas; symbols indicate the color of yarn. The easiest and most practical method is to buy a pre-stamped canvas which has the design printed in colors to match the yarn.

The latch hook and yarn

The wooden handle latch hook used for Smyrna stitch is very comfortable and works rapidly. A small latch or tongue on the hook is opened and shut by the passage of the yarn through the canvas holes.

The rug in the large picture has been worked in a traditional Persian design using an all wool rug yarn. Above: A picture of the stamped canvas and packages of pre-cut rug yarn.

How to work Smyrna stitch

Rugs are worked one knot at a time, moving from left to right (or vice versa, if handier) in successive rows. Contrary to needlepoint, you must never skip from one color area to another. The most comfortable position for working is from the bottom to the top so that the finished rows lie in your lap. If you wish to work on a table, as in the photographs, you will have to anchor the upper edge of the canvas with heavy weights. However, most rug weavers prefer to fold the canvas on the line of holes to be worked and the latch hook passes through both canvas holes automatically. Place all the colors of yarn to be used in a convenient position for you to reach while working.

The method of knotting is clearly illustrated. Step 1: insert the open latch hook down under the strand of canvas and out of the hole above. Step 2: with

The latch hook is essential for smyrna stitch. Below: step 1 of the knotting.

your left hand fold a strand of yarn evenly over the shank, bringing the yarn under the hook and over the latch; pull the hook towards you, holding on to the yarn until the latch closes. Step 3: release the yarn and pull hook back through canvas holes and loop of yarn. Step 4: pull ends of yarn taut to tighten the knot.

Above: Step 2 of the knotting. Below: Step 3. To the right: The knot has been tightened in step 4.

Proceed in this manner along each row, keeping an even tension on the knots, until the canvas has been filled. Before starting the rug, fold the excess at edges under and work the outer rows through both thicknesses of the canvas for a smooth, finished edge. When the canvas is completely covered, trim away any irregular ends with sharp scissors.

THE PATCHWORK AFGHAN

The patchwork afghan, made of left-over yarns, is the grandmother of all lap robes, commonly called "The Granny Afghan." This is worked in separate squares of solid or multi-colored yarns; each one always is finished off with a last row of one main color which becomes the background. The squares are joined on the wrong side with an overcast stitch and may be trimmed with a knotted fringe when finished. These colorful, simple squares are not restricted solely to afghans in today's fashion world; they are also used to make pillows, casual skirts, ponchos, etc. Use your own creativity and the instructions for the squares on page 144.

KNITTING

Knitting is a more demanding needlecraft than crocheting; it is a mathematical science subject to many rules and regulations. The truly expert knitters may camouflage a sharp, analytical mind under a sweet domesticated smile!

At any rate, even if knitting is a strict, though rewarding experience, learning how to knit properly can be a very pleasant adventure. Mastering the complicated formula of an elaborate pattern stitch generates a true feeling of accomplishment. Every knitter who successfully completes a professional looking dress or coat wears upon it the medal of perseverance.

Since you are already familiar with the asterisks and terminology of crochet, we shall now expand that knowledge and explore the wider field of knitting, assisted as before with self-explanatory pictures.

BASIC PRINCIPLES OF KNITTING

Knitting requires a different technique than crocheting and also a knowledge of certain basic principles which we shall now explain.

Selecting the needles

Needles are always chosen in proportion to the type of yarn you plan to use. Knitting needles range from the smallest, in size 0, to the larger needles, in sizes up to 15.

1

2

Casting on with one needle: picture 1: the yarn is placed over the thumb and index finger while the right hand regulates the tension. Picture 2: starting the first loop.

Very fine baby or zephyr yarns would require number 2 or 3 needles, sport yarns numbers 4 through 6, knitting worsted numbers 7 through 10, and the heavier bulky yarns use the 13 to 15 size range. The needle size must always be adjusted to meet specific requirements for gauges and row count.

Knitting a gauge

A small sample of the stitch you plan to use must always be knitted on approximately 20 stitches before starting a garment. This sample, or gauge,

is necessary to determine the exact number of stitches per inch knitted by the individual knitter; an essential element in calculating the correct number of stitches with which to start the garment.

3

4

Picture 3: the right hand inserts the needle and throws the thread to form the loop. Picture 4: first loop, or stitch, on needle.

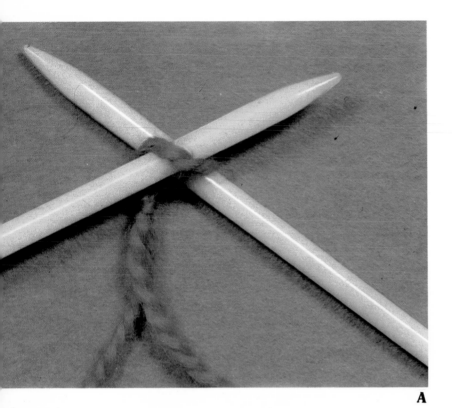

Casting on stitches

Knitting is started with a cast on row which may be done with either one or two needles.

Casting on with one needle
(*Illustrated on pp. 162-163*)

Fig. 1.
Measure off a long strand of yarn from end of skein, make a slip knot and place on needle.

Fig. 2.
Wrap free end of yarn over left thumb and index finger to form loop, hold yarn from skein in right hand and insert needle in loop.

Fig. 3.
Wrap yarn around needle and draw thread through loop over thumb.

Casting on with 2 needles: pictures A and B illustrate first 2 steps of procedure.

Fig. 4.
Tighten gently to form a stitch.

B

Casting on with two needles

Fig. A opposite.
Make slip knot and place on left hand needle; insert right hand needle into loop.

Below and on the opposite page: the 3 steps of casting on with 2 needles. This does not require two threads for casting on.

C

Fig. B opposite.
Wrap yarn over right hand needle and draw out a loop.

Fig. C above.
Twist loop and transfer to left hand needle, gently tighten thread and start next stitch by inserting right needle in last stitch.

How to knit

Knitting proceeds from right to left, working one stitch at a time onto the right hand needle. Insert right hand needle into first stitch on left needle, wrap yarn over point of needle and draw out a stitch onto the right needle.

Position of the hands

Proper position of the hands while knitting is essential for well regulated stitches. The needle containing the stitches is held in the left hand and the right hand wraps the yarn. In order to maintain even thread tension, wrap the yarn around the little finger of your right hand, up over and around the index finger. With a little bit of experimentation and practice, your hands will automatically hold the needles and feed the yarn properly.

Below: the proper position of hands holding the needles and wrapping the yarn.

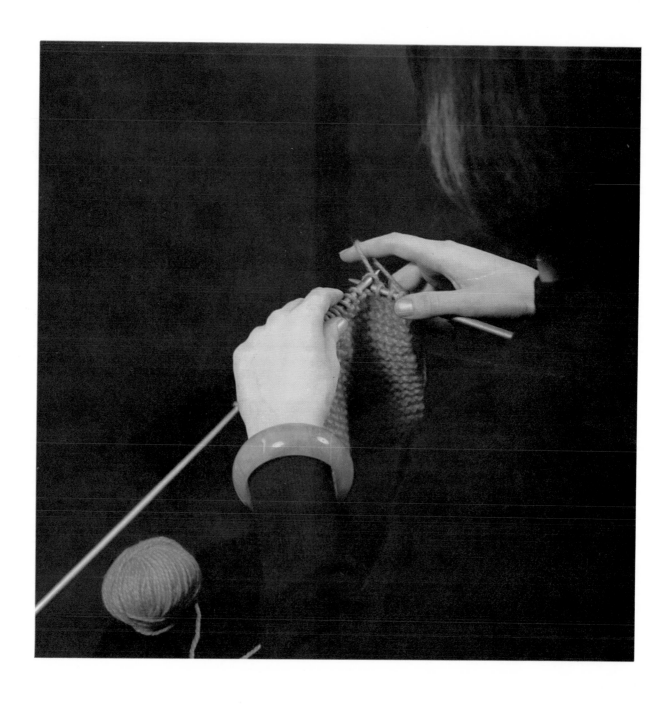

ABBREVIATIONS
AND
EXPLANATIONS

- **Crochet stitches**

Ch -	chain
Sc -	single crochet
Hdc -	half double crochet
Dc -	double crochet
Yo -	place yarn over hook for extra loop
Sp -	space
Rnd -	round

- **Knitting stitches**

K -	knit
P -	purl
Tw -	twist 2 sts by knitting the second before the first
Yo -	yarn over, place yarn over needle for extra st
Ea -	each
Prev -	previous
St -	stitch

- **Explanations**

Repeat bet *'s	repeat the directions written between the two *'s across the entire row
Psso -	pass the slipped stitch over the one just knitted
Sl st -	slip stitch, slip stitch to right needle without knitting it
Dec -	decrease by working 2 or more sts. together
Inc -	increase by knitting in front then back of same stitch

(Picture 1) Multiple of 4 plus 3. Row 1: *K 2, P 2*; repeat bet *'s ending K 2, P 1. Repeat this row for pattern.

(Picture 2) Multiple of 4. Rows 1, 9 & 13: *K 2, P 2*; repeat bet *'s. Row 2 and all even rows: Follow the sts on needle. Rows 3, 11 & 19: p 1, *K 2, P 2*; repeat bet *'s ending P 1. Rows 5 & 17: *P 2, K 2*; repeat bet *'s Rows 7 & 15: K 1, *P 2, K 2*; repeat bet *'s ending K 1. Repeat 20 rows for pattern.

(Picture 3) Multiple of 4. Row 1: *K 2, P twist 2 (purl st and leave on needle, purl first st and drop loops f needle)*; repeat bet *'s. Repeat this row for pattern.

(Picture 4) Multiple of 8 plus 1. Row 1: P 3, *K 3, P 5*; peat bet *'s ending P 3. Row 2: K 4, *sl 1 as to P, K 7*; peat bet *'s ending K 4. Repeat two rows for pattern.

URED PATTERNS

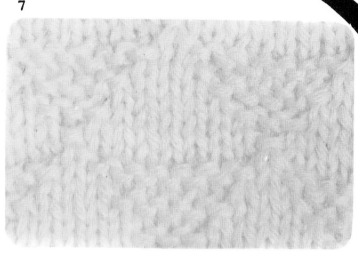

7

5

6

(Picture 6) Multiple of 2. Row 1: *K in back of 2nd st and leave on needle, K first st, drop both loops*; repeat bet *'s. Row 2: *P 2nd st and leave on needle, P first st and drop loopw*; repeat bet *'s. Repeat these two rows for pattern.

(Picture 7) Multiple of 8 plus 1. Row 1: K 1, *P 7, K 1*; repeat bet *'s. Row 2 and all even rows: Purl. Row 3: K 2, *P 5, K 3*; repeat bet *'s ending K 2. Row 5: K 3 *P 3, K 5*; repeat bet *'s ending K 3. Row 7: K 4, *P 1, K 7*; repeat bet *'s ending K 4. Row 9: P 4, *K 1, P 7*; repeat bet *'s ending P 4. Row 11: P 3, *K 3, P 5*; repeat bet *'s ending P 3. Row 13: P 2, *K 5, P 3*; repeat bet *'s ending P 2. Row 15: P 1, *K 7, P 1*; repeat bet *'s. Repeat 16 rows for pattern.

(Picture 8) Multiple of 6. Row 1 & 7: Knit. Rows 2 & 6: Purl. Rows 3, 4 & 5: *K 3, P 3*; repeat bet *'s. Roes 8, 9 & 10: *P 3, K 3*; repeat bet *'s.

8

ture 5) Multiple of 8 plus 1. Row 1: P 1, *K 7, P 1*; re-
bet *'s. Row 2 and all even rows: Follow sts on needle.
s 3 & 15; K 1, *P 1, K 5, P 1, K 1*; repeat bet *'s.
s 5 & 13: K 2, *P 1, K 3*; repeat bet *'s ending K 2.
s 7 & 11: K 3, *P 1, K 1, P 1, K 5*; repeat bet *'s ending
. Row 9: K 4, *p 1, K 7*; repeat bet *'s ending K 4. Re-
16 rows for pattern.

TWO SPORT SWEATERS

Pictured here are two easy-to-knit sport sweaters using the cable stitch you will learn on page 179. If you do your homework, it should be very easy for you to knit either one of them. Use sport yarn with #4 needles and a #3 needle for the K 1, P 1 ribbing around neck, cuffs, and bottom border. Cast on a multiple of 22 stitches and set pattern on right side as follows: K 5, *P 2, K 8 (cable), P 2, K 10*; repeat bet. *'s, ending K 5. On the wrong side, follow back the stitches; twist the cable every 12 rows, starting the first twist after 6 rows. Refer to all the shaping and figuring directions in this chapter and happy knitting!

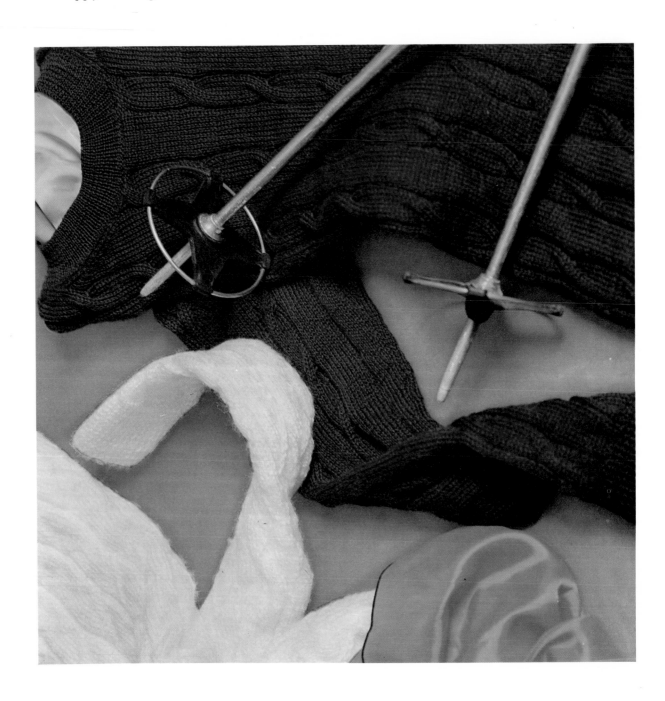

THE BASIC STITCHES

Knitting consists of two basic stitches, the knit and the purl. All pattern stitches are a combination of the two worked in various ways.

How to knit

With yarn in back, insert point of right needle through stitch on left needle, wrap yarn over point and draw stitch out.

How to purl

With yarn in front, insert right needle from right to left through front of stitch on left needle, wrap yarn around point and draw stitch out.

Below: forming the knit stitch with yarn in back. On the right: the purl stitch with yarn in front.

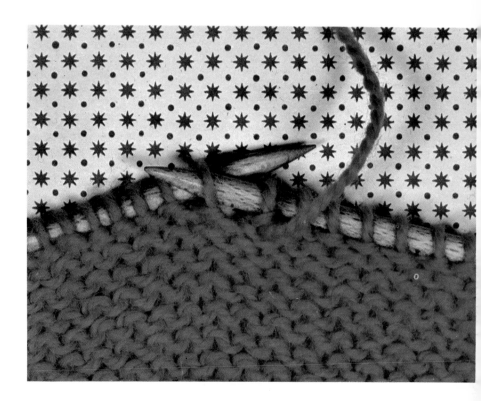

Above: on the left, stockinette stitch; on the right, purl side of stockinette. Below: on the left, garter stitch; on the right, seed stitch.

The four knitting textures

There are four basic textures to knitting which comprise the foundation of all knitted articles; each is a combination of knit and purl stitches.

● Stockinette Stitch - Alternately knit one row and purl one row.

● Purl side of Stockinette - Wrong side of stockinette stitch; used to separate cables, raised patterns and ribbed stitches.

● Garter Stitch - Knit every row; this is used on scarves, borders and any garment which must be reversible.

● Seed Stitch - K 1, P 1, reversing to P 1, K 1 on the next row; this stitch is also reversible.

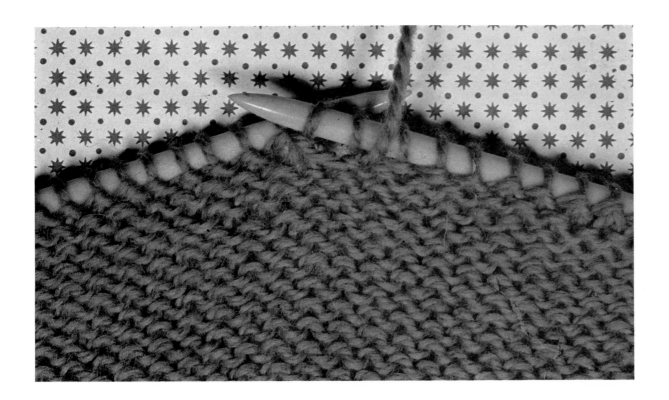

How to work twisted knit stitch

Insert needle in back loop of stitch instead of front and wrap yarn same as plain knitting.

How to work twisted purl stitch

Insert needle in back loop of stitch, twist needles slightly and purl in regular way.

Twisted knitting and purling is the first variation on the two basic stitches. Above: the twisted purl. Below: the twisted knit.

THE MOST FREQUENTLY USED STITCHES

This is a group of stitches with precise requirements as each one has a specific function. It is essential that you understand them and master the technique of each.

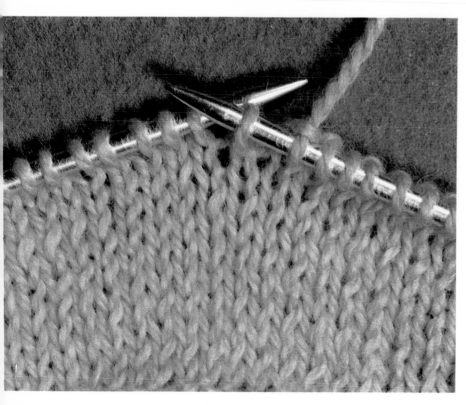

On the left: slipping a knit stitch with yarn in back; slip the purl stitch with yarn in front. Below: passing the slipped stitch over.

Slip stitch (sl st)
To slip a stitch, simply lift it off the left needle with right needle and do not work it. When instructions say "slip as if to K", keep yarn in back of work; "slip as if to P" means to keep the yarn in front of work.

Passing the slipped stitch over (PSSO)
This is used in many pattern stitches and for decreasing. Slip the next stitch on needle, knit the next stitch and reach back with left needle to lift the slipped stitch over the knitted stitch and drop off needle.

Yarn over (YO) on the knit side

The yarn is wrapped over the right needle, from back to front, after knitting a stitch, in order to add a stitch, replace a stitch, or make an eyelet in the pattern. On the next row it is worked in the usual way.

Above: on the left, the yarn over on knit side; on the right, yarn over on purl side. Below: PSSO from the left.

Yarn over (YO) on the purl side

After purling the stitch, wrap yarn over needle and bring it to front of work; on next row, work in usual way.

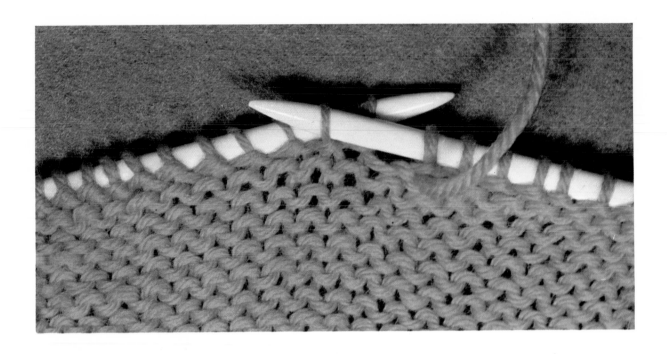

*In the picture above: twist stitch on the purl row.
Below: knitting in the row below.*

How to work the twist stitches

This is a method of knitting used in pattern stitches
and some cables. On the knit side of the work, to
make a left twist, knit the second stitch in the back
and leave loop on left needle, knit the first stitch
and drop loops; for a right twist, knit in front of
the second stitch, keep loop on needle, knit the
first stitch and drop both loops.

How to work the purl twist

This is an easier stitch; purl in the front of second
stitch and leave on needle, purl first stitch and
drop both loops.

How to work double stitch

This stitch is also used for pattern effects. Insert
needle in stitch of row below and knit in normal
manner.

SOME ATTRACTIVE PATTERN STITCHES

These are stitches which utilize unorthodox techniques or supplementary tools. In addition to those in the previous group, they create many unique textures and patterns.

How to work elongated stitches

This stitch is very similar to the one we covered in the crochet section, although the technique is obviously different. It is worked only on stockinette as follows: insert point of right needle in stitch, wrap yarn around it 3 times and draw yarn through. On the following row, work 1 loop of the stitch, dropping extra wraps.

Below: wrapping the yarn 3 times for elongated stitches in first step.

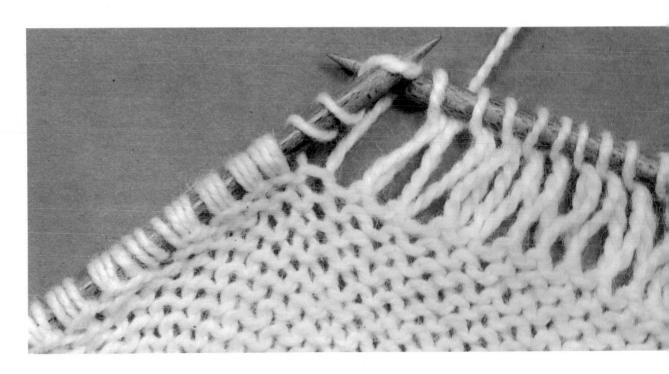

Above: step 2 of elongated stitches on second row. Below: a very pretty application of elongated and crossed stitches.

How to work elongated and crossed stitches

Elongated stitches, plus the technique of crossed stitches, create a very unusual pattern stitch. The directions are as follows: cast on a multiple of 8 stitches and knit 8 rows. On the 9th row, work elongated stitches wrapping the yarn 3 times. Row 10: (Crossover Row) Before starting the row, *slip 8 stitches to right needle dropping the extra wraps, replace on left needle and knit the 5th, 6th, 7th, and 8th stitches passing each one over the needle as shown in picture, then knit the first 4 stitches*; repeat between *'s across row.

How to lengthen stitches with a hook

Another version of elongated stitches presents a totally different effect. This is also worked on the right side of stockinette stitch. Work across row to place marked for lengthened stitch, insert crochet hook 4 or 5 rows below, draw up a long loop, place on left needle and work together with next stitch unless this stitch is to be added to a pattern. It is also possible to draw up the loop without a hook by inserting right needle into stitch, wrapping yarn in back and drawing out the long loop.

How to work raised bubble stitch

This is a most effective application of lengthened stitches which creates a raised, textured bubble on the flat surface of stockinette. Cast on a multiple of 6 stitches and work stockinette stitch for 1 inch. On the right side of work, *K 6 sts, insert hook bet 6th and 7th sts 4 rows below and (draw up a loop to place on left needle, YO on left needle) 4 times, K all loops together with next st *. Continue in this manner, placing a bubble between every 6th and 7th stitch. Work 1 inch stockinette, work bubbles on next row, starting first one between 3rd and 4th stitch, thus alternating the bubbles.

Above: the lengthened stitch ready to be worked off the needle. Below: using a crochet hook to form the raised bubble.

How to work cable stitches

Cables have always been the backbone of truly handsome sport sweaters for both men and women. Although cables appear to be complicated, the use of a double-point cable needle simplifies the work to a point where even a beginner can venture. It is very worthwhile to learn the simple technique of handling a third needle. The cable twist is worked as follows: Work to the point marked for cable, place first half of cable stitches to double point (dp) needle and hold in front (left twist), knit the second half of cable stitches, knit the stitches from spare needle; continue across row to next cable band. The right twist is worked exactly the same way, holding the first half of cable stitches in the back instead of front. There are many cables which use both right and left twists to create unusual patterns.

How to work horizontal bubbles

This is another textured stitch which utilizes the cable needle. Work across the right side of work to point marked for bubble, place the next 3 stitches on a double point needle and wrap yarn around these 3 stitches as many times as necessary for the desired texture, then knit the 3 stitches from spare needle and continue across row to place marked for next bubble.

Additional interesting applications of the cable technique will be found on pages 184 and 185.

Above: position of cable needle for a left twist.
Below: a horizontal bubble using the cable needle.

THREE IDEAS FOR DINNERTIME

Baby bibs are charmingly attractive and a simple enough project for any beginner. Basic bib: with fingering yarn and #3 needles, cast on 70 sts and work in stockinette for 10 inches. On next knit row, work across 22 sts, attach another ball of yarn and bind off 26 sts; finish last 22 sts. Working both sides at once, continue to stockinette on each piece for 2 more inches and bind off. Work 1 row single crochet completely around outer edges; make 2 chains 10 inches long and attach to corners of neck edge for ties. After knitting the first one, try a pattern stitch or stripes as pictured below; the variety is endless.

INCREASING AND DECREASING

There are several routine shaping techniques which every knitter must learn in order to interpret printed directions correctly or to improvise on her own.

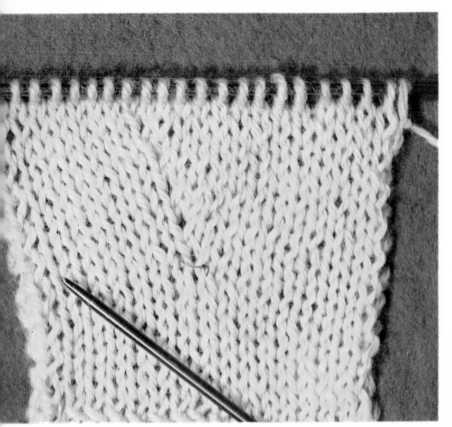

Decorative increasing

An attractive, openwork increase pattern uses the same method as above, with one exception; place a yarn over on the right needle at the marker instead of increasing in the stitch. On the next row, work the yarn over as a stitch. Another method is to pick up the thread between the stitch and the marker, twist thread and place on left needle, then work it in normal way on next row.

On the left; plain increasing within the row. Below: openwork increasing using a yarn over.

Increasing at the sides

To increase 1 stitch at side edges, work in the front, then back of the first stitch and next to last stitch. If more than one stitch must be increased at sides on same row, place needle in first stitch and use two-needle cast on method explained previously, until the desired number of stitches has been added.

Increasing within the row

When increases are to be made within a row, place a marker on the needle at designated point and increase in the stitch next to the marker on every other or every 4th row.

Decorative decreasing

On raglan shapings and certain pattern stitches, a special effect is required. For the raglan shaping, K first 2 or 3 stitches, K next 2 tog, work to within last 4 or 5 stitches, work 2 tog in back loops, finish last stitches. Another method is as follows: K 1, pass 3rd st on left needle over first 2 sts, K 2 tog, YO and continue across row to within last 4 sts; YO, sl 1, K 2 tog, PSSO, K 1. A twist stitch is another decorative method to use. Work to within 5 sts of end of K row, K 3rd and 4th st tog in back, K the skipped st; on purl side work the same way using a purl twist instead of a knit twist.

On the left: a simple raglan decrease. Below: decorative decrease using twist stitches.

Decreasing at the sides

To decrease one stitch at sides, simply knit the two end stitches together. If more than one stitch is to be decreased, use a bind off and slip the first stitch instead of knitting it to avoid a very jagged edge.

Decreasing within the row

This is accomplished in the same way as decreasing at ends. Two or three stitches are knitted together; for a left slant knit the stitches together in back, and for a right slant work them together normally.

Note: To cable left, place first half of cable group on d[ouble] point (dp) needle and hold in front of work; kn[it] second half of cable group, knit the first half fro[m] needle. To cable right, work same as left cable, ho[ld] first half of cable group in back instead of front.

(Picture 1) Cast on 16 sts for sample gauge. Row 1: P 2, K 12, P 2. Ro 2 and all even rows: Follow sts on needle. Row 3: P 2, place 4 sts on dp needle and hold in back, K 4, K sts from dp needle, K 4, P 2. Row 5: P 2, K 4, place next 4 sts on dp needle and hold in front, K 4, K sts from dp needle, P 2. Repeat rows 3 - 6 for pattern.

(Picture 2) Cast on 16 sts. Row 1: P 2, K 12, P 2. Row 2 and all even rows: Follow sts on needle. Row 3: P 2, cable 3 sts right, K 3, cable 3 sts left, K 3, P 2. Rows 4 through 10: Follow sts on needle. Repeat rows 3 - 10 for pattern.

(Picture 3) Cast on a multiple of 12. Row 1: Knit. Row 2 and all even rows: Purl. Row 3: *Cable 3 sts left, K 9*; repeat bet *'s. Row 5: Knit. Row 7: *K 6, cable 3 sts right, K 3*; repeat bet *'s. Repeat rows 3 - 8 for pattern.

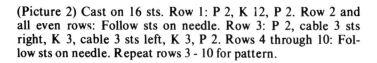

(Picture 4) Multiple of 7 plus 4. Row 1: P 4, *K 3, P 4*[; re]peat bet *'s. Rows 2, 3 & 4: Follow sts on needle. R[ow 5:] P 4, *K 3rd st in front and retain on needle, K first st, K [2nd] st and drop loops off needle; P 4*; repeat bet *'s. R[epeat] rows 2 - 5 for pattern.

~AISED STITCHES

(~icture 5) Multiple of 6 plus 1. Note: WYIF - with yarn in ~ont, WYIB - with yarn in back. Rows 1 & 7: Purl. Rows ~ & 8: Knit. Rows 3 & 5: K 1, *WYIF sl 2, WYIB K 4*; re-~eat bet *'s. Rows 9 & 11: *K 4, WYIF slip 2*; repeat bet ~ ending K 1. Rows 4, 6, 10, 12: Purl, slipping the slipped ~ of prev row.

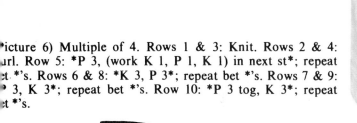

(Picture 7) Multiple of 6 plus 1. Rows 1 & 3: *P 1, K 5*; re-peat bet *'s ending P 1. Row 2 and all even rows: Follow sts on needle. Row 5: * (P 1, sl next st to cable hook and hold in front, sl next 3 sts to another cable needle and hold in back, K the 5th st, then 3 sts from cable needle, K first st from hook in front), P 1, K 5*; repeat bet *'s ending P 1. Row 7: Same as row 1. Row 9: *P 1, K 5, repeat bet ( ) of row 5*; repeat bet *'s ending P 1. Repeat rows 1 - 10 for pat-tern.

(Picture 8) Multiple of 6 plus 3. Note: To make knot stitch, K1,P1,K1,P1 in next st (as if increasing), turn, K the 4 sts, turn, P the 4 sts, turn, WYIB pass the 3 extra sts one at a time over the first one.
Rows 1, 3, 5: Knit. Rows 2, 4, 6, 8: Purl. Row 7: K 4, *work knot st in next st, K 5*; repeat bet *'s ending K 4. Rows 10, 12, 14, 16: Purl. Rows 9, 11, 13: Knit. Row 15: K 1, repeat bet *'s of row 7, ending K 1.

~icture 6) Multiple of 4. Rows 1 & 3: Knit. Rows 2 & 4: ~url. Row 5: *P 3, (work K 1, P 1, K 1) in next st*; repeat ~ *'s. Rows 6 & 8: *K 3, P 3*; repeat bet *'s. Rows 7 & 9: ~ 3, K 3*; repeat bet *'s. Row 10: *P 3 tog, K 3*; repeat ~ *'s.

A LEGGING SET

A pretty legging set (like the one shown below) is a classic for mothers and grandmothers to knit while waiting for the new baby to arrive. Within the pages that follow, you will learn all the techniques and details necessary to complete one with ease. If you have admired hand knitted garments on babies in the past, now is the time to attempt one. Pick out an appealing style in a favorite baby book, follow the line and measurements, and apply any of the decorative stitches taught here to create contrasting yokes and collars, borders and sleeve detail.

STYLING AND SHAPING

There are certain fundamental techniques for shaping necklines, inserting pockets, working in buttonholes, etc., which you must learn and understand in order to complete a garment successfully.

How to work vertical buttonholes

Knitting buttonholes into the work uses the same method as crochet. Attach a second skein of yarn to the stitch which must be separated for the opening, and work both sides at once until opening is same length as diameter of button. Fasten off second skein of yarn and continue to work in one piece.

How to work horizontal buttonholes

On the right side of the work, bind off as many stitches as necessary for button to pass through and finish row.

On the right: one side of a vertical buttonhole (worked separately for photographic reasons). Below: a rounded buttonhole.

On the return row, cast on the same number of stitches over the bound off ones and continue to work normally.

How to work round buttonholes

This type of buttonhole is only suitable for very small buttons. On the right side of work, yarn over, knit the next two stitches together and finish row. On the wrong side, work the yarn over as a regular stitch.

How to work vertical pockets

Vertical pockets are made very similarly to vertical buttonholes. Prepare a pocket lining as above and place on spare needle. Mark the garment at point of pocket opening, work from seam edge over to opening and place front half of work on holder, pick up pocket lining and continue across these stitches. Work seam edge of garment with pocket lining until desired height for opening; bind off the stitches added for pocket lining and place rest on holder. Pick up front piece which was left on holder and work the same number of rows as on seam edge; join to stitches on holder and work as one piece. After finishing garment, sew lining to body on inside.

On the left: inside view of horizontal pocket with lining. Below: pocket border sewn to right side. On the right: V neckline without border.

How to work v necklines

Divide the work at center on same row as armhole. Bind off and decrease at each side of neck edge. The frequency of neckline decreases is determined

by the number of rows from underarm to shoulder which can be counted on the back section of the garment. Knit 2 stitches together (at the edge or several stitches inside the edge), either on every other or every fourth row, depending on the number of rows in the armhole and the number of stitches to be decreased to shoulder edge. The neck border is added afterwards by picking up stitches along the neck edge and working a K 1, P 1 ribbing. Work the center stitch at point of V as a knit stitch on the right side and decrease 1 stitch each side of this one on every other row of border.

How to work rounded necklines

First, determine the number of stitches to be used in neckline shaping. Work to within 2 inches of top of shoulder and shape neck; in center of row, bind off half the number of stitches for neck shaping, leaving 1/4 of the number with each shoulder. Attach another ball of yarn and, working both sides at once, decrease one stitch each side of neck edge every other row until reaching shoulder edge, then begin to bind off shoulder stitches also. For a stockinette border, sew the front and back of one shoulder together and, with right side facing, pick up the stitches all around the neck edge. Work 1 inch of stockinette, purl one row on right side of

The rounded neckline (below) and cap of sleeve (on the right) are both decreased with precise calculations.

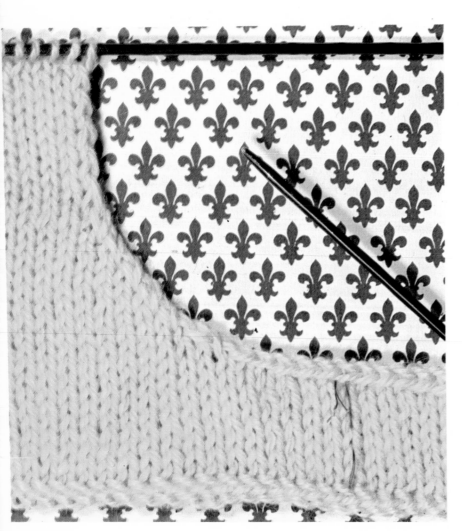

work for turning ridge, then work 1 more row of stockinette and bind off loosely. Fold along purl row after sewing other shoulder and tack loosely to inside neckline edge.

How to work the ribbed neckband

If you wish to work a neckline ribbing without seams, pick up the stitches around neck edge and divide on four double-point needles. Use a fifth needle to work K 1, P 1 ribbing and bind off loosely in ribbing.

How to sew the shoulders

The graduated method of binding off a shoulder leaves a jagged edge which is difficult to sew neatly. The most satisfactory technique is to place the pieces right sides together, and backstitch a straight line with the same yarn along an upward slant as close to the bound off stitches as possible.

How to work the sleeve cap

The most common type of sleeve is the set-in sleeve. Raglan or kimono sleeves must be shaped to conform to individual styling; we will, therefore, only discuss the set-in sleeve. After the sleeve has been worked up to underarm, bind off one inch of stitches at each side. The cap is shaped with decreases as follows: decrease one stitch at the beginning and end of every other row for a distance 1/2 the armhole measurement, then bind off two or three stitches at the beginning of the next four rows; bind off the remaining stitches on the next row. For a very heavy arm, the stitches should be decreased less frequently.

How to work vertical darts

Darts are necessary on bodices when a heavy bust would pull the garment out of shape, and on skirts to decrease the hip fullness to the waistline measurement. For bust darts, place a marker at a point approximately 4 inches from each side seam and increase before and after each marker every 4 - 8 rows (depending on the number of additional stitches necessary) until one inch below the underarm. On skirts, divide the work into thirds and place a marker to separate each section; decrease one stitch before and after each marker every 6 - 8 rows, depending on the number of decreases necessary.

How to work horizontal darts

This type of dart is generally used on the bodice of a dress for a figure with a rather heavy bust. The method used is a technique called "short rows" started approximately one inch below the underarm. Tie a thread marker to a stitch four inches from each side seam and work short rows as follows: with right side facing, work to within one inch of side seam, turn and work to within one inch of other seam, turn and work to within two inches of side seam, turn and work to within two inches of other seam. Continue in this manner until short rows reach the markers, remove markers and begin to work across entire row again. The bodice will now show a definite fullness at center.

Above: the horizontal dart is indispensible for a well fitting dress, especially in the case of a heavy figure.

THE CHRISTENING DRESS

Even the most modern mother, who spends her pre-delivery days reading up on child psychology and proper nutrition, likes to knit something for the baby while waiting. Perhaps you have gazed longingly at pictures in baby books illustrating dresses similar to the ones pictured below. Choose a style in a simple stitch and don't be afraid to attempt it; they may look complicated, but shaping baby knits is relatively simple, and you will find everything you need to know within the pages of this chapter. Use a soft baby or fingering yarn and a number 2 or 3 needle for an elegant baby dress.

HELPFUL FINISHING DETAILS

The quality of a knitted work is obviously dependent upon more than just a perfectly executed stitch; it must also be finished well. There are several finishing details which you will find beneficial in future endeavors.

How to work borders

When the borders of necklines, pockets, etc., are to be added after the garment is finished, they will look much more professional if they are picked up instead of being worked separately and then sewn to the garment. To pick up stitches along the edge of your work, use a crochet hook to draw a loop out of the stitch and place it on a knitting needle, one stitch at a time. After picking up the stitches, use a ribbing stitch, garter stitch or seed stitch, whichever is best suited to the overall style of the garment.

Below: the flat fold-over hem which gives a smooth finished edge.

How to work hems

There are several different ways to treat the hemline of a garment when it is not started with a K 1, P 1 ribbing. For a flat, fold-over hem, work stockinette for one inch, purl one row on the right side for a turning ridge and continue in stockinette or pattern stitch. After finishing, the hem is sewn to the garment on the wrong side with small, loose stitches.

Another method, which gives a rolled hem, is to work two inches, fold one half to the inside and work the next row by inserting the needle into the stitch on left needle and through one loop of the cast on stitch in back. The picot hem is worked in stockinette for one inch; on next right side row, * K 2 tog, YO*; repeat across row. Purl the next row and continue in regular stitch. After finishing, fold hem to the inside on the eyelet row and slip stitch in place on the wrong side.

In the picture above, the picot hem. Below: the rolled hem which is joined while knitting.

How to bind off

If a bound off edge is pulled too tightly, the seam will pucker after sewing. To bind off properly, when passing one stitch over the other, take care to keep the thread slack or use a larger needle. When binding off ribbing, you must bind off with knits and purls in order for the edge to retain its elasticity.

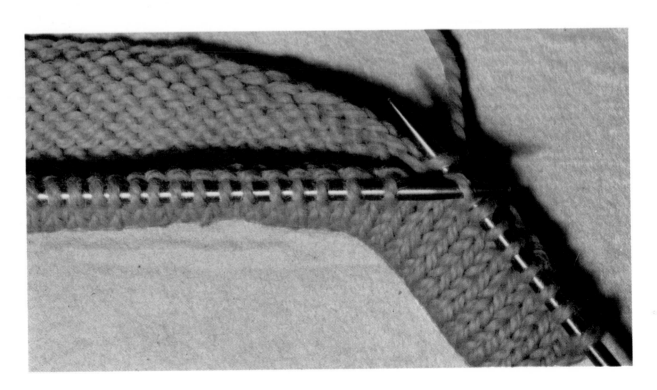

How to work selvages

Never underestimate the importance of selvages. Irregular edges will result in an irregular seam; on edges which will not be joined to others, the work must not curl or pull. Here are three techniques, each one for a specific purpose.

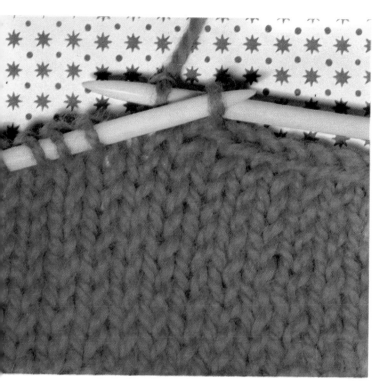

● Chain selvage - Used as a trimming on the sides; slip the first stitch, purl the second, work across row to last two stitches, purl one and slip the last stitch. Purl these stitches on the wrong side.

Above: simple selvage. Above right: pearled selvage. Below: chain selvage.

● Pearled selvage - Used on edge stockinette stitch to avoid curling; slip the first and knit the last stitch on knit side and purl side. Another version is just to slip the first stitch on every row.

● Simple selvage - Used on any edge which will be joined to another; knit the first and last stitch on each row.

WARM AND COLORFUL MITTENS

*Are you ready to knit a pair of mittens for that precious child? Here is a basic pattern which you can follow or interpret with your favorite stitch. You will need one skein of knitting worsted and needles in sizes 3 and 5. With #3 needles, cast on 40 sts and work K 1, P 1 ribbing 3 ins. increasing 2 sts along last row. Change to #5 needles and stocki-nette for 1 in. ending after purl row. K first 10 sts and place on holder for thumb. Work remaining 32 sts in stockinette for 2 ins. ending after purl row. Dec row: *K 3, K 2 tog*; repeat across row and purl back. Second dec row: *K 2, K 2 tog*; repeat and purl back. Third dec row: *K 1, K 2 tog*; repeat and purl back. Fourth dec row: K 2 tog all across row; break off yarn leaving a long end, draw through all sts with a blunt wool needle twice. Pull tog tightly and sew up outer edge. Place 10 thumb sts on needle and work stockinette for 1 1/2 ins. K 2 tog across next row; fasten off and sew seam same as side of mitten. When dividing for thumb on second mitten, leave last 10 sts on holder.*

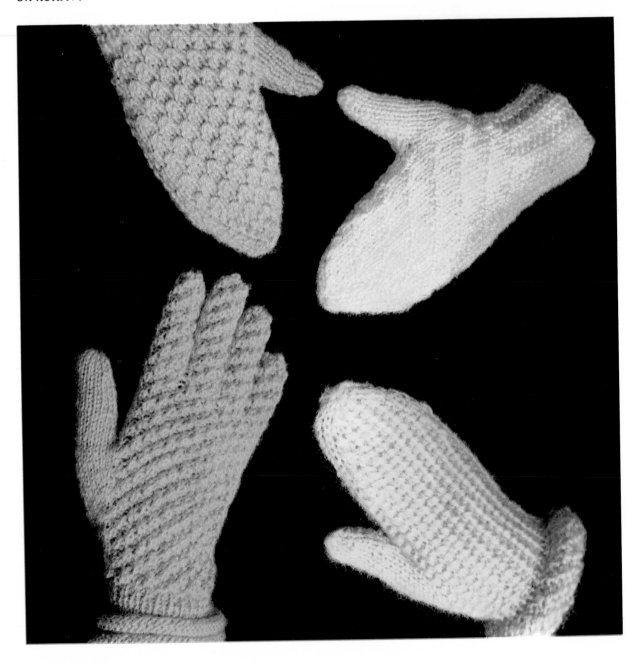

THE JACQUARD TECHNIQUE

Jacquard type of knitting requires patience and skill; however, mastering its techniques will provide innumerable rewards in future knitting ventures. As your skill increases, working argyles and fabric patterns can be accomplished with unexpected ease.

The design

Jacquard knitting is generally restricted to stockinette stitch with several colors worked into a design. A graph is always necessary and the method is the same as for needlepoint: i.e., each square represents a stitch and each symbol a color. In order to avoid tangling the skeins of different colors, it is best to buy a set of yarn bobbins which are sold in all needlework departments. Use the skein of the background color and wind the contrasting colors on the bobbins.

How to work large motifs

There are two different techniques in working with colors: one is suitable for large designs and the other for very small designs which are uniformly spaced and create a fabric look. If the design has large areas of color, it is possible to use a skein

Below: changing colors in back of the work for jacquard knitting.

Above: crossing the threads on the purl side of work.

of yarn, instead of a bobbin, for each color. The threads must be crossed when changing colors in order to lock the stitches together and avoid holes between stitches. The threads are crossed by bringing the new color underneath the color being dropped; when this crossing is completed on both sides of the work, all stitches will be automatically locked.

How to work small motifs

If the areas of color are very small and closely spaced, it is possible simply to carry the colors along the back of the work. However, when using this technique, care must be taken to allow enough slack in the carried thread to avoid pulling the stitches, and the threads must still be crossed in back to avoid holes in the work. In the case of widely scattered tiny motifs, or the vertical lines of a plaid, it is better to embroider them with a duplicate stitch after the large areas are completed.

AN ELEGANT BEDSPREAD

Here is a spread destined to become a cherished heirloom. Each square is made of 4 triangles sewn together. Use fingering yarn and a number 2 or 3 needle. Row 1: Cast on 3 sts and K 1, YO, K 1, YO, K 1. Row 2: Inc in first st. P 3, inc in last st. Row 3: P 1, YO, place marker on needle, K 2, YO, K 1, YO, K 2, place marker on needle, YO, P 1. (Sts bet markers are leaf pattern). Row 4 and all even rows: Follow sts on needle. Row 5: P 1, YO, P to marker, K 3, YO, K 1, YO, K 3, P to last st, YO, P 1. Row 7: P 1, YO, P to marker, K 4, YO, K 1, YO, K 4, P to last st, YO, P 1. Continue in this manner adding 1 st to ea side of purl section and 1 st on ea side of center of leaf until there are 21 sts bet markers. Continue to inc 1 st at ea edge of triangle while decreasing 1 st ea side of leaf inside markers until 3 sts remain on leaf on next right side row, P the 3 sts tog. Continue to inc at sides for entire triangle while working 2 more rows of stockinette, reverse next 2 rows of stockinette, work 4 more rows stockinette as before. Work 10 rows of eyelet pattern (K 2 tog, YO all across right side row and purl on wrong side), then 4 rows of stockinette as before, reverse 2 rows of stockinette, then begin leaf pattern on next row, spacing 6 leaves evenly across row. After leaf closes, work 2 rows stockinette, reverse 2 rows, 4 rows as before and bind off.

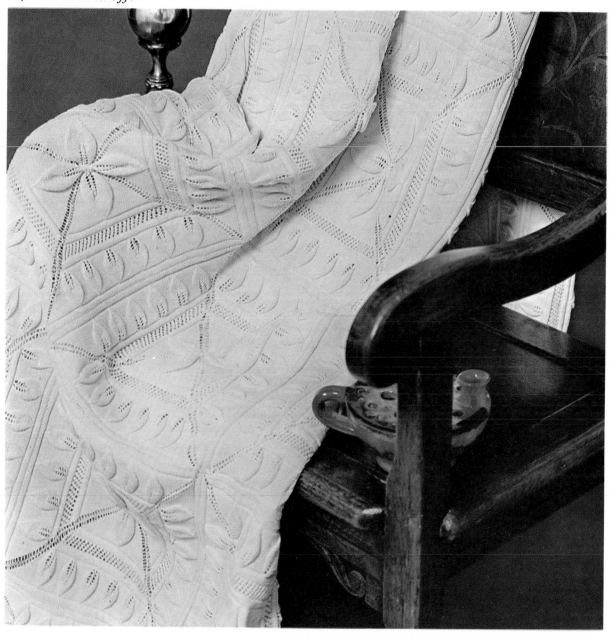

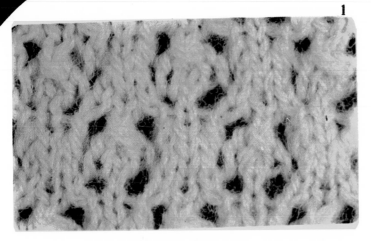

1

(Picture 1) Multiple of 6 plus 2 for seam sts. Row 1: K 1, *K 1, YO, sl 1 K 1 PSSO, K 1, K 2 tog, YO*; repeat *'s, ending K 1. Row 2 and even rows: Purl. Row 3: K 3, *YO, K 3*; repeat bet *'s ending K 2. Row 5: K 1, K 2 tog, *YO, sl 1 K 1 PSSO, K 1, K 2 tog, YO, sl 1 K 2 tog PSSO*; repeat bet *'s ending YO, K 2 tog in back. Row 7: K 1, *K 1, K 2 tog, YO, K 1, YO, sl 1 K 1 PSSO*; repeat bet *'s ending K 1. Row 9: Same as Row 3. Row 11: K 1, *K 1, K 2 tog, YO, sl 1 K 2 tog PSSO, YO, sl 1 K 1 PSSO*; repeat bet *'s ending K 1. Repeat rows 1 - 12 for pattern.

(Picture 2) Multiple of 10 plus 1. Row 1: K 1, YO, *K 3, sl K 2 tog PSSO, K 3, YO, K 1, YO*; repeat bet *'s ending YO, K 1. Row 2 and all even rows: Purl. Row 3: K 2, YO, *K 2, sl 1 K 2 tog PSSO, K 2, YO, K 3, YO*; repeat bet *'s ending YO, K 2. Row 5: K 3, YO, *K 1, sl 1 K 2 tog PSSO, K 1, YO, K 5, YO*; repeat bet *'s ending YO, K 3. Row 7: K 4, YO, *sl 1 K 2 tog PSSO, YO, K 7, YO*; repeat bet *'s ending YO, K 4. Row 9: K 2 tog, K 3, *YO, K 1, YO, K 3,

sl 1 K 2 tog PSSO, K 3*; repeat bet *'s ending YO, K 1, YO, K 3, K 2 tog. Row 11: K 2 tog, K 2, *YO, K 3, YO, K 2, sl 1 K 2 tog PSSO, K 2*; repeat bet *'s ending YO, K 3, YO, K 2, K 2 tog. Row 13: K 2 tog, K 1, *YO, K 5, YO, K 1, sl 1 K 2 tog PSSO, K 1*; repeat bet *'s ending YO, K 5, YO, K 1, K 2 tog. Row 15: K 2 tog, *YO, K 7, YO, sl 1 K 2 tog PSSO*; repeat ending YO, K 7, YO, K 2 tog. Repeat rows 1 - 16.

3

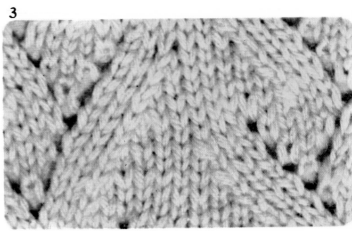

4

(Picture 3) Multiple 16. Row 1: *K 3, K 2 tog, K 2, YO, K 5, YO, K 2, sl 1 K 1 PSSO*; repeat bet *'s. Row 2 and all even rows: Purl. Row 3: *K 2, K 2 tog, K 2, YO, K 1, YO, K 2, sl 1 K 1 PSSO, K 5*; repeat bet *'s ending K 7. Row 5: *K 1, K 2 tog, K 2, YO, K 3, YO, K 2, sl 1 K 1 PSSO, K 4*; repeat bet *'s. Row 7: *K 2 tog, K 2, YO, K 5, YO, K 2, sl 1 K 1 PSSO, K 3*; repeat bet *'s. Row 9: *K 5, K 2 tog, K 2, YO, K 1, YO, K 2, sl 1 K 1 PSSO, K 2*; repeat bet *'s. Row 11: *K 4, K 2 tog, K 2, YO, K 3, YO, K 2, sl 1 K 1 PSSO, K 1*; repeat bet *'s. Repeat rows 1 - 12 for pattern.

2

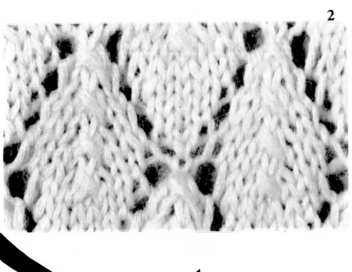

COLORED STITCHES

(Picture 4) Multiple of 6. Rows 1 & 5: Purl. Rows 2 & 6: Knit. Row 3: K 2 wrapping yarn double, *sl 2, K 4 with double wrap*; repeat ending K 2 with double wrap. Row 4: Purl across dropping the extra loop of double wrap and slipping the slipped sts of prev. row. Row 7: Sl 1, *K 4 with double wrap, sl 2*; repeat ending sl 1. Row 8: Same as row 4. Repeat rows 1 - 8 for pattern.

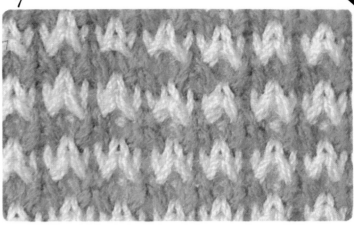

Row 3: Color B, K 1, *K 1 in row below, sl 1*; repeat ending K 1. Row 4: Purl, slipping the slipped st of prev. row. Row 5: Knit. Row 6: Purl. Repeat rows 1 - 6.

(Picture 7) Multiple of 3 plus 1. Use 2 colors; alternate every 2 rows. Row 1: *K 2, sl 1*; repeat ending K 1. Row 2 and all even rows: Purl. Row 3: K 1, *sl 1, K 2*; repeat bet *'s. Row 5: K 3, *sl 1, K 2*; repeat ending K 3. Repeat rows 1 - 6 for pattern.

(Picture 8) Multiple of 7. This is a jacquard type of stitch; carry yarn in back and cross when changing colors. Work in stockinette, starting with a knit row; pattern is for color changes. Row 1: 2 green, *1 orange, 6 green*; repeat ending 4 green. Row 2: Purl, following back colors. Row 3: *2 green, 5 orange*; repeat. Row 4: *2 green, 3 orange, 1 green, 1 orange*; repeat. Row 5: 1 green, *4 orange, 3 green*; repeat ending 2 green. Row 6: 2 green, *1 orange, 6 green*; repeat ending 4 green. Row 7: 4 green, *1 orange, 6 green*; repeat ending 2 green. Row 8: Purl, following back the colors. Repeat rows 1 - 8 for pattern.

(Picture 5) Multiple of 4. This is a 4 row pattern in 3 colors; change colors every 2 rows. Row 1: Color A, *K 3, sl 1*; repeat bet *'s. Row 2: *Sl 1, K 3*; repeat. Row 3: Color B, K 1, *sl 1, K 3*; repeat ending K 2. Row 4: K 2, *sl 1, K 3*; repeat ending K 1. Rows 5 and 6; Use color C and begin to repeat pattern from row 1.

(Picture 6) Any even multiple. Use 2 colors; 2 rows of color A, 4 rows of color B. Row 1: Color A, Knit. Row 2: Purl.

DECORATIVE TOUCHES

We have assembled a few simple suggestions for trimming your work. Although they are not knitting techniques, per se, you will find them to be priceless knitting tricks.

How to work duplicate stitch embroidery

Duplicate stitch is worked exactly like a lazy daisy stitch in embroidery. Thread a blunt tapestry needle with yarn and bring needle out of the center of stitch below the one you wish to embroider, pass the needle from right to left under the two threads of the stitch above and bring the needle back down into the original stitch. If you are embroidering more than one stitch in a vertical line, bring the needle out again in the center of the finished stitch.

This is a simple, rapid technique for jacquard patterns with small, scattered motifs and vertical lines on plaids.

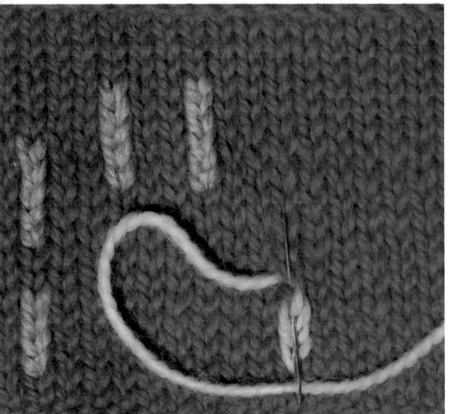

On the left: movement of the needle in duplicate stitch. Above: smocking with yarn on purl ribs.

How to work smocking

The knitted version of the classical honeycomb smocking is also worked the same way as in embroidery. You must knit the foundation first; *P 3, K 1* across the right side of your work and follow back the stitches on the wrong side. The ribs are then smocked with two horizontal stitches as pictured.

How to work pompoms

Pompoms are widely used as trimmings on many items. They are very easy to make even though the finished product looks difficult.

Pompom makers can be purchased in any needlework department; however, if you choose to make your own, here is how it is done. Cut two cardboard circles the size you wish the finished pompom to be, then cut a small hole about the size of a dime in the center of each one. Measure off approximately 6 strands of yarn, 2 yards long; hold

All the steps to make a pompom are shown in the pictures below and on the right.

the two cardboard discs together in your left hand and wind the strands of yarn through the hole and around the rim as pictured. The quantity of yarn used will determine the fullness of the pompom. Insert a sharp scissors carefully between the two cardboard discs and cut the yarn all around. Separate the discs slightly, take a strand of yarn 12 inches long and wind around the cut strands (between the discs) twice and tie tightly. Remove the discs and trim any stray ends.

How to work tassels

Tassels are another decorative trimming detail which are extremely popular and very simple to make. Cut a cardboard rectangle approximately 2 inches wide and the desired height for finished tassel. Wrap the yarn around the cardboard as many times as is necessary for the size tassel you wish, then thread a blunt tapestry needle with a double strand of the same yarn. Pass the needle under all the strands at the top of the tassel, tie a tight knot and make a loop for hanging; cut the threads at the bottom, then wrap the thread several times around the cut strands to form the head of the tassel, knot, and pass the needle down through the center. Trim any stray ends with a sharp scissors.

Above: the two steps in making a tassel. Below: a very lovely woolen scarf, heavily trimmed with tassels.

ASSEMBLING THE GARMENT

This is the actual moment of truth for any knitted garment. It is the final phase in which the knitting must be tailored properly. A knitted fabric is harder to handle than cloth and its tailoring, naturally, must be modified to fit specific requirements.

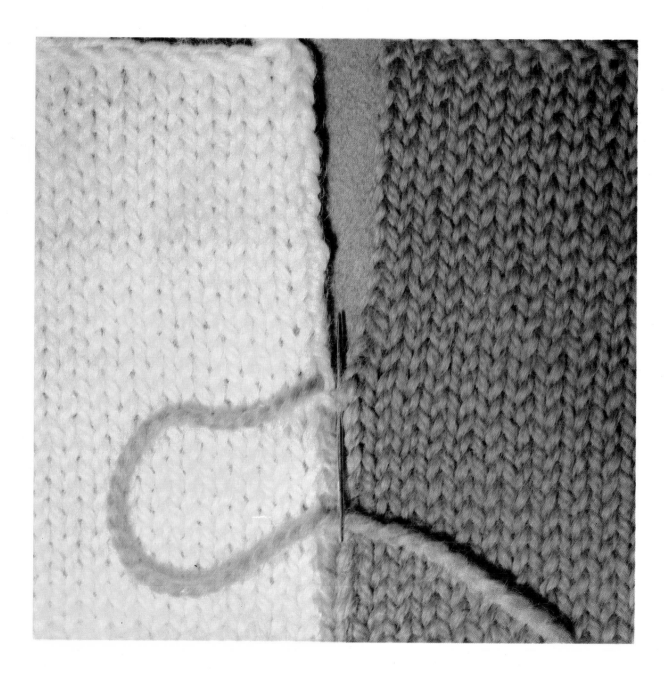

Knitted pieces are seamed with a different method than sewing on fabric. They may be joined on the wrong side with a back stitch, or woven on the right side. The picture above illustrates the duplicate stitch weaving method which gives an invisible seam.

Using a pattern

In order to avoid an ill fitting garment when finished, it is wise to use a pattern guide while working. The guide may be a paper pattern, an old well-fitting skirt or sweater which has been taken apart, or you can make a basic fitted pattern with a piece of muslin. Most large paper pattern companies make a basic fitted pattern in all sizes which is available in pattern departments of all department stores. The muslin fitted pattern is truly the best method, as even the most perfectly written knitting directions do not provide for individual figure requirements such as a heavy bust, sloping shoulders, short underarm to waist measurements, etc.

Steaming or blocking

The steaming or blocking operation is indisputably the most delicate and essential phase of any knitted work. It is in this phase that some irregularities may be corrected, and improper handling may cause a disaster. If you adhere meticulously to the precise directions which follow, there will be no room for error. Pin the pieces to a large, well padded board in the exact shape of the guide you used while knitting. Do not be too lazy to move and adjust the pins several times wherever necessary. Place identical pieces, such as sleeves and fronts of sweaters, with right sides together, on top of one another. Cover with a very wet cloth and pass the iron lightly and evenly over the cloth. Do not allow the weight of the iron to rest on the knitted pieces; steam alone is sufficient to do the pressing job. If the yarn is one which cannot be steamed, such as lamé, chenille or ribbon, follow the same method but do not use the iron. Instead, wet the cloth to excess and pat the moisture into the knitted pieces with your hands. Allow to dry thoroughly before removing from board.

In the final analysis though, it is wise to remember that no amount of blocking will correct a garment which was knitted too large or too small. The first washing will return it to the original dimensions.

On the right: a dropped stitch may be picked up with a crochet hook which does not necessitate ripping the work.

Seams

After blocking, the pieces are joined together with one of three seaming methods as follows:

● Back stitch: When the pieces to be joined have irregular edges, as in the case of shoulders and set-in sleeves, the best method is to back stitch with the same yarn in a tapestry needle, as close to the edge as possible.

● Duplicate stitch: In the case of two pieces which are to be joined in a definitive manner, as a decoration or plaid, the two pieces are placed side by side and a duplicate stitch is worked between the end stitch of each piece as illustrated on page 205.

● Weaving: This method provides a completely invisible seam and is worked from the right side. Hold edges together and bring needle up through first stitch on left edge; insert needle down through center of first stitch on right edge and pass-under the knot out to the right side. Continue to work from side to side in this manner, always passing the needle under the knot.

Dropped stitches

Dropped stitches may be picked up with a crochet hook; insert hook in stitch and draw horizontal thread in back through to front and place on needle.

Lining knitted garments

Very often knitted garments need to be lined, either for a specific effect or to add body to the work. Choose a fabric which is light in weight but not too soft to hold its own shape; stiff taffetas and faille will not conform too well to the knitted fabric. Draw a paper pattern the same size and shape as each piece of knitting before assembling the garment. When ready to cut the lining, be sure to remember that the knit fabric will give in places where the lining will not; therefore, cut the lining with an extra allowance for fullness across shoulder, back, and bustline darts, as well as with seam allowances. Stitch the lining to the garment with small hand stitches around armholes, neck and fronts, if open. The lower edge must be hemmed and allowed to fall free. A skirt lining is made separately, hemmed, and attached to knitted skirt around waistline and along sides of placket opening.

SPORTY KNEE–HI'S

These are two-needle socks worked quickly and easily with any sport yarn and a number 3 needle, using your favorite stitch. Cast on the number of stitches necessary for individual calf measurement and work decreases in the length from knee to ankle until 46 sts remain. Place 12 sts at ea end of needle on holders for heel and work center 22 sts for 6 ins; dec 1 st ea side every other row 7 times and place remaining 8 sts on holder. Transfer the 24 heel sts to one needle and work as one piece for 2 1-2 ins. Turn heel: Work 6 sts, 2 sts, tog, work 8 sts, 2 sts tog and turn without finishing the row. *Sl 1, work 8 sts, 2 tog turn*. Repeat bet *'s until all side sts have been decreased. Pick up 10 sts along ea side of heel and place on needle. Continue to work, decreasing 1 st ea side every 4th row 6 times, then every other row 7 times. Weave the toe sts tog and sew up the back leg seams.

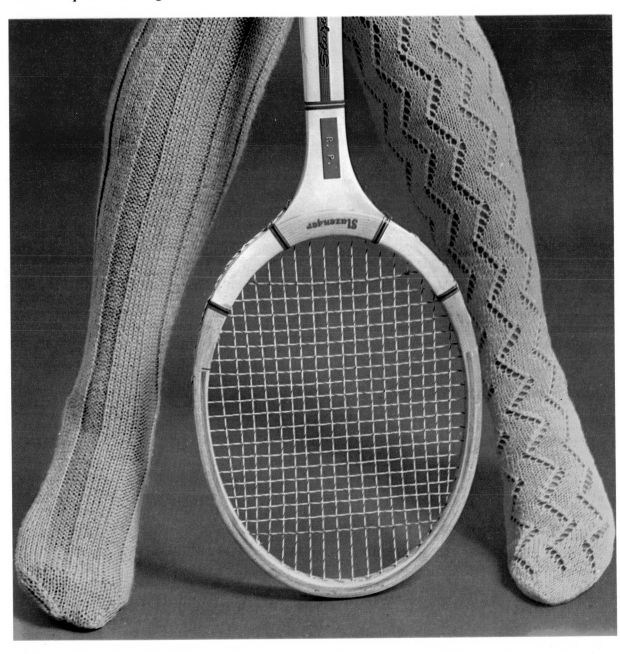